Testimony

Any trial that you may have had to overcome....

Early in my career in the military, it was a struggle because of my race. As a Private E-1 it was hard they didn't want to promote the black Soldiers, but they worked the hell out of us. When I was station in Germany as Private First Class, I had a 1st Lieutenant that refused to promote and reenlist me because I wouldn't kiss his ass like the white Soldiers. Being from Chicago and growing up in the hood, I wasn't taking it. I stood my ground and went to the Battalion Commander. The Commander promoted and reenlisted me.

Another thing that I had to overcome is dealing with losing one of my Soldiers and one of my fellow First Sergeants while serving in Iraq along with multiple injuries to a few of my other Soldiers due to our unit coming under fire of rockets coming into the camp from enemy forces. These casualties and injuries weigh very heavily on my heart and mind. As a result, I have struggled with Post Traumatic Stress Disorder, Anxiety and Depression. Even today when I read about Soldiers killed in action it takes me back to the loss of my Soldier and colleague. I thank God above for my wife, my family, and friends that pray for me and love me and help to keep me focused.

Being in the Army for 30 years it was a struggle at trying to balance work/family. I was away from my family very often and it was extremely difficult to adjust or find where I fit in when I returned home. I had to pray very hard to control my frustrations and not feeling like I belonged when I would return home after a long deployment or training exercise. My wife had to be the mother and the father in my absence. She had to be the nurturer and the disciplinarian and it was hard for me to just right into their routine knowing that it wouldn't be long before I had to leave. It was hard for me to communicate or interact in a loving manner with my wife and kids after losing my Soldiers as I was so used to interacting with my Soldiers. I often just wanted to be alone when at home. It was hard for my wife and kids to understand my actions as no knew the pain that I was holding inside. This lead to a domestic incident that I am not proud of. An event that pushed my family and me further apart mentally, emotionally and physically. Thank God that we were able to overcome all of this and come together again after my retirement.

I am very proud of my wife taking the time out of her life and sharing her story as a Soldier. I have worked with many females over the years and I've seen first -hand the racism, the gender bias, hostile work environment and overall mistreatment of many female Soldiers and civilians. Being a Senior Non-Commissioned Officer, it was my job to counsel, protect and impart wisdom of how to overcome the many adversities of serving your country while black. Being married to another service member, I have witnessed my wife overcome many of these struggles at various commands. I think it is very needed for her to use her voice and create a platform for others to do the same by sharing just a piece of their testimony to make the way for other a little easier.

Anthony Smith
Sergeant Major, Retired

Overcoming a Military traumatic experience ....

In 1998 while stationed at Ft Stewart Ga, my unit deployed to Kuwait. Shortly after we got boots on the ground and settled into our area of living, we began our platoon training with our 120mm Mortar system. About 2 weeks later, we started out to our objective in order to conduct our Platoon live-fire exercise. I was designated as the lead track vehicle. I conducted all pre-execution checks, mapped out location and route (basic land navigation) and also ensured the coordinates were accurate in my plugger. We began movement to our objective- about 30 minutes into our convoy, we made a quick stop and I rechecked my grid coordinates, etc. Everything looked on point except I felt uneasy about the direction of travel.

Again, I was told to continue the mission. As I was leading our Platoon across this humongous open dessert, I spotted a convoy of vehicles speeding our way- at this point, I alerted the Platoon Leader & Platoon Sergeant. We were told to man our 50 caliber and M16's and take up security positions. As the convoy approached we noticed it was friendly along with Range Control and Kuwaiti Police Force. They ask who was in charge and have us all get out of our vehicles. Here is the issue, they informed us that we were traveling across a live-fire zone. The Artillery unit utilizing the range spotted us before they began their 2nd iteration of fire missions.

They asked who was the lead track and I responded. I was asked what steps did I take preparing the convoy and I showed them my plotted map points & plugger etc. After the Kuwait Police checked, they reported that the plugger had malfunctioned and calculated the wrong grid and direction. My plotted direction on my map was correct but I trusted a computer with the lives of twenty-four Soldiers. The Kuwait Police escorted out of the live-fire zone- and informed the Battalion Commander of the incident and conducted a full-fledged investigation. Range Control and the Kuwaiti police advised us that if the Artillery Soldier had not spotted us, it would have been a friendly fire fratricide.

I've been living with the thought that I almost got my entire Platoon killed. Several white guys in my Platoon blamed me and we had a big fallout between some of the guys that we call brothers. There were racial comments being tossed around, several Soldiers requested to transfer to other units and some Soldiers got completely out of the Army because of that incident. I was always told it wasn't my fault but that was not the answer to this issue that continues to haunt me. I've held this guilt and shame in for over ten years and finally, I had to get help. The dreams and anything that reminded me of the event caused me to shut down or try to avoid situations and people. My anger, communication issues, and antisocial personality put serious stress on my family to where I almost lost everything. With the support of my friends & family, I'm definitely in a better place. Today, I continue to see my therapist and take medication to help deal with the trauma-induced Post Traumatic Stress, Depression and Anxiety. As an Africa-American man in the Army, I have faced many issues aside from the events mentioned above. I have had to deal with racism up close and personal. I have been called a nigger to my face and had to keep my composure. I think it's great for God to place it on her heart to share a little of her story and create an outlet for others to heal through the sharing of their testimony.

Danny W.
Sergeant Major Retired

UNLEASHING THE ROAR

I AM MY SISTER'S KEEPER

A COMPILATION BY
KATHY R. SMITH

Unleashing the Roar

FIRST EDITION

Book design by Allison Arnett of www.branditbeautifully.com

ISBN 978-0-578-65731-8

Scriptures are from the King James Bible unless otherwise
indicated.

Dedication

This book is dedicated to all of the African- American female Soldiers, Sailors, Airmen, Marines and the Coast Guard that may suffer in silence as a result of life experiences and experiences from their military service. This book is dedicated to all of the African- American female Soldiers, Sailors, Airmen, Marines and the Coast Guard that may come behind us. You don't have to suffer any more. You don't have to be ashamed of who you are, where you come from, what you look like or what you've been through anymore. The power is on the inside of you. Your experiences make you stronger, use your voice as a platform to heal from your past and to heal those around you. There is power is your praise, let your light illuminate for all to see you bold, beautiful, intelligent black woman!

– Kathy R. Smith

Table of Contents

Foreword

While reading the personal histories accounted in Unleashing the Roar, I was initially uneasy at allowing the stories to regurgitate my own traumatizing memories of my military service. I had hidden these memories from my family, friends, and even myself for a purpose. I firmly believed that sharing these memories would somehow –perhaps inadvertently- mask my successful career as a high-ranking officer in the military and instead associate me as only a victim. I had believed the lies that the hate generated toward me through discrimination was due to my own failure for being an African American woman. What lies! While reliving memories was painful, this book reminded me that I share these experiences with my fellow African American brothers and sisters who have served and still serve in the military. I was reminded that we are not victims or failures for the color of our skin, but we are strong and victorious human beings by the nature of our character.

I served 28 years in the US Army, and I am now a retired US Army Colonel and combat veteran. During my tenure in the US Army, I supported V11 Corp while assigned to a 300 Bed Combat Support Hospital during Operation Desert Shield and Desert Storm. I joined the military with the sole purpose of fighting for and serving my country. I can say that I served my country with all my heart and passion, but I can't say I enjoyed the experience. I met many wonderful people along the way and had some great experiences, but I still lived through the majority of my career in a heightened level of stress to constantly prove myself. Through my experiences, I better understood the covert nature of discrimination - it is organized and lethal to many careers. The systems in place to protect the innocent are ran and governed by the offenders.

Despite the discrimination I faced during my service, my motivation to always represent my best-self earned me honors and the rank as a senior officer. While my peers and fellow soldiers may view my career in the military as a success, they do not see the full history of discrimination that haunted my career. My career was full of roadblocks established through the longstanding culture of discrimination in the military.

I have long held-back the memories of my military past until I read Unleashing the Roar. What I love about this book is its pure representation of good soldiers who, like me, endured great pain while serving their country. Unleashing the Roar validates the difficulties I faced in the military due to discrimination and affirms that I am not alone in the constant battle against discrimination. Kathy Smith is one of those good soldiers who also fights in the battle.

I had the pleasure of meeting Kathy in the Buffalo Soldiers Motorcycle Club (BSMC) where we are both members. We both joined the club to enjoy the comradery of fellow African American veterans with similar service experiences. But we also joined the club to continue the legacy of the Buffalo Soldiers 9th & 10th Calvary Regiments and the first (and only) African American woman (Cathay Williams) enlisted in the Buffalo Soldiers, who served their country from 1866 to 1948 (when Harry Truman disbanded segregation in the military). Through the club, we regularly volunteer to serve our community and share our stories to instill hope in those who endure discrimination.

In addition to BSMC, Kathy has dedicated her passionate life to help others. She navigates women through the trenches of life and has established non-profit programs to help young girls and underserved individuals. She dedicates this book to the many African American soldiers who suffer by discrimination in silence so they may all know that they are not alone in their suffering. Her purpose in life is to pave the way for our next generation of African Americans to find success while thwarting the power of discrimination that destroys lives.

I wish I could say this book accounts for the many successes we have gained in the military to disband discrimination; unfortunately, this book affirms that discrimination lives on to crush the marginalized. This books accounts for the sexual assault, domestic violence and many other issues suffered by these women while in uniform. While that may seem counter-productive for an inspirational read, the intention of the book is to share the harsh truth of reality despite how painful it seems. The intention of this book is to document the history of discrimination in the US Military during the 20th and 21st centuries and to provide validation for soldiers still suffering from the damage discrimination caused to their careers. Because of this book, no one can hide that discrimination is alive and well in the US military.

Despite the unprecedented evils Kathy and I faced in the military, we both used our life trials to retire from the military as better individuals. Instead of falling victim to our pain, we became stronger and willed ourselves to fight back. We did not fight back with hate but with love. While we have not yet defeated the system that rewards discrimination, we fight it by building up the next generation of African Americans who live through their convictions and virtues to serve and protect the marginalized. We have learned that you cannot fight hate with hate.

While I may not see discrimination end during my time left on this earth, I hope many individuals will take courage in the stories documented in Unleashing the Roar. I hope these stories empower you to survive. You can still make a difference through your service to our country – whatever that service may be for you. Do not keep silent about your traumas but share them with love so that you may heal while also encouraging others who battle with hidden pain.

As the great Martin Luther King, Jr once said, "I have decided to stick with love. Hate is too great a burden to bear."

Karen Chambers
Colonel, Retired USAR

I Am My Sister's Keeper

BY KATHY R. SMITH

What in the hell? If you had told me that I was going to experience sexual assault, domestic violence, racial ethnic hatred, gender bias and hostile work environment while serving in the military I would have laughed SGT Alston out of my face when he approached me my junior year of high school about joining the Army. Truth be told I would have asked him, "Why in the hell would you recommend someone to join an organization like that? Honestly, I guess those things could happen anywhere. The military is comprised of individuals from all walks of life with various backgrounds, ethnicities and upbringing. While I endured some "stuff" in the military, it brought about many benefits, life changing experiences and memories that have molded the women that you see today.

Nearing the end of my AIT (Advanced Individual Training), I was assigned to attend Postal School to pick up working in the post office as an additional skillset to my current profession as an Administrative Specialist. Yes, I was a Soldier and in addition to training for combat readiness my everyday job was an Administrative

Specialist. Prior to AIT ending our battalion began getting weekend passes off post. Some of my female battle buddies and myself would use our weekend passes to go shop and enjoy night life as a way to reward ourselves for nearing the end of our training and getting a sense of normalcy. Many of us entered the military immediately after high school graduation. We left family and friends at home and took an oath to protect and defend our nation whiles our fellow high school peers were at home partying and preparing for college or just celebrating the completion of their high school years. Anywhere from four to six of us that didn't have family come up on the weekends would go off-base and share the cost of a hotel room. We would get a room in a location close to shopping and restaurants as none of us had cars in the training environment. We enjoyed local night clubs, comedy clubs and just resting without having to get up and clean the barracks, or march to and from chow. We partied and had a great time. However, one morning after a night of hitting the local clubs a few of us woke up very hungry and decided to walk across the street to McDonalds and grab breakfast. I remember it like yesterday, Sims, McKnight and myself were walking across the street and this car went by with a light-skinned man with the prettiest eyes that I had ever seen. We locked eyes and exchanged stares as he went by and me and my friends crossed the street. He quickly turned around and met us at McDonald's. He got out of the car and Lord help me. He stood 6'0 about 160lbs with gorgeous eyes and a smile to match. You see he was fine, but so was I. I stood 5'7, 140lbs and the smoothest dark brown skin you could imagine with a natural beauty mark just above my top lip and could rock a sundress or a pair of jeans and Timberlands snatching the attention of most men without an ounce of effort. Ron gave me his number, paid for our food and I promised to call him. You see, back then we didn't have cell phones. Most people had beepers but in training we couldn't have that.

We ladies returned to our hotel and later on I gave Ron a call. He and his brother came and hung out with us for a bit and gave us a ride back on post. I had three weeks of training left and I would talk to Ron occasionally on the phone when I got a chance. After standing in line to use a payphone, I usually tried to call home and speak with my grandparents, my mom and sisters. After graduating AIT I moved a few buildings down to Charley Company. This is where the permanent party stayed when they had training. Thank you Jesus! It was official, I was a Soldier in the United States Army and had completed my Basic Training and Advanced Individual Training. As a permanent party, I had a lot more freedom and flexibility than I had experienced as a trainee. We had our physical fitness formations at 0600 and reported to school from 0800 – 1700. After the school day you could come and go as you pleased. I met a handsome young man by the name of Williamson. Umph...he was so fine. Tall, light-skinned, slim with brown eyes and a gorgeous smile. Had men been hiding before or was I so bogged down with getting through my basic and AIT that I was too busy to notice? Either way, being single and away from home and on my own for the first time these fellas were certainly catching my attention. I began to hang out with Williamson who was also in Charley Company however he was near the end of his training. He was a very respectful, intelligent young man. I was eighteen and he was twenty-four. At the end of our duty day we would hang out in his room and talk and watch movies for hours. I often fell asleep with him caressing my scalp as he ran his fingers through my hair. He had to leave for his next duty station before we could even see what a relationship would have been.

After Williamson left, I remembered Ron. I called him from the payphone after work and he eagerly agreed to pick me up and hang out. How could I have forgotten about him.He pulled up to pick me up and we would go to dinner, happy hour with some of my battle buddies from class or hang out with his family. I was having so much fun finally living life on my terms that the safety briefings given by our drill sergeants about always traveling in a group and avoiding certain areas completely eluded me. Ron and I began enjoying each other's company. He began picking me up after work every day. I began spending the night with him where he lived with his aunt and brother. One night we fell asleep on the floor watching television. It was November in Columbia, SC and snow had fallen outside and it was cold. I woke up to him caressing my breast and sucking on my neck. We began kissing and his kisses and caressing moved lower down my body, from front to back. What came next was obvious, he entered me and was still so gentle still kissing along my neck and ears. Right there on that living room floor where anyone could have walked by, it was happening. We had to be quiet to keep from waking anyone else. I was caught up and so was he. We were like Bonnie and Clyde. Sometimes I would sneak him in and he'd spend the night with me at the barracks. My roommate was cool with it. Ron brought his brother and introduced him to my room-mate and they hit off as well. One-night Ron had to make a stop, as he came to get back into the car the police pulled up and shined their light on us. I had no idea what was going on as I had never been stopped by the police before. They spoke to him outside the car and then came to the car to see who was inside and look at my identification. They asked me what we were doing in the area and I advised that he had just picked me up from Ft. Jackson and he stopped to see a friend. They spoke with Ron and someone else outside and eventually let us go. It may have lasted about twenty minutes but seemed like forever. Ron came back to the car and someone got in the back seat behind me. He said that he had to give them a ride. I was quiet and they talked and he thanked them for covering for him. When the other person got out, I couldn't believe it! I grew up in the hood, I knew what a crackhead looked like! I realized that Ron's profession was street pharmaceuticals. It all made sense, he was always in different cars and always had to stop somewhere. No wonder he was always available whenever I called.

I should have cut his ass off the minute I realized what he did for a living. Not to mention that every time I got in that car with him, I put my life and my career in jeopardy. We were having so much fun hanging with one another, his family my roommate and the sex....Lord I wanted to walk away but I couldn't break away. A few days later we were driving through town and this car began following us, blowing the horn and driving crazy trying to get him to pull over. He sped up and we were in the midst of racing through town to get away from this crazy driver. He told me it was his ex-girlfriend.....ladies don't fall for this mess. I later found out that this so-called ex-girlfriend was pregnant with his kid. Thankfully, my additional few weeks in Columbia, SC had come to an end. I received orders to report to Korea, after graduating from postal school. Ron was devastated but I promised to stay in touch and told him things would work out.

I left Ft. Jackson and went home on two weeks leave just in time to spend Christmas and New Year's at home with my family before boarding a flight headed to Korea. *They say hindsight is 20/20, that's no lie. If I could go back and talk to my younger self, I would make sure that she knew that it's okay to party and have a good time, but to practice abstinence or at best, safe sex always! I would tell her of the consequences of unprotected sex. We would discuss sexually transmitted diseases, soul ties and genetics. You see pregnancy isn't the only risk of unprotected sex. When a baby is formed, there is a joining of DNA. If there are things about your mate that you don't like or you don't know such as family medical history, you will get to know these things up close and very personal. That child doesn't have to spend a single day of their life in the presence of their other parent to look like them, to act like them, think like them or to develop illness or disease that may run in the other parent's life. Things like ADHD, autism, addiction, diabetes, hypertension, mental illness, cancer and a host of other diseases could plague your child throughout their life. If I could educate young men and women on anything before I get to the joys and pains and benefits of military service, my talks would certainly include sexual awareness, education, the importance of choosing your partners wisely, always using protection until you have taken the time to really get to know your mate and their family. This way you can make an informed decision about childbirth prior to forming a seed with someone* that you may not want anything to do with after the fact.

Coming home for the holidays was exciting; I made it home just in time for Christmas. I got a chance to see my mom and my sisters. Grandma made it down from Ocala. My family cooked a feast and it was just like old times. My Grandma was like an Oracle of my time. The woman knew everything about everything, she could look at you and know everything about you before you opened your mouth and said a single word. As I was walking her out, she looked at me and said, "Your hips sho' nuff spreading." I had this weird look on my face and asked Grandma "Seriously, are you calling me fat? Thinking all this running and exercising that I've been doing there's no way. I had exercised and hydrated so much there were times that I threw up water. There was no way that I was fat. She looked back and said, "No, you're not fat, but your hips...time will tell." I hated when she didn't finish her sentence, I knew that that something was on her mind and she was always right. I had no idea what she meant at that time, but she couldn't have been more correct. Time would certainly tell, and it didn't take much time at all. Unfortunately, my stay at home was very short. I had to be in Korea right after the new year.

I reported to Korea as ordered. Korea wasn't a bad assignment at all. It was cold, but not bad. I was stationed in Camp Coiner working in Postal Operations until moving over to Kimpo, the main airport still working in the postal service. Postal was a very demanding job, so I didn't have a lot of down time during the day or on the weekends. We worked shifts, so on my off days, I usually hung with the people from my shift that were also off. We were a small unit and treated one another like family. One thing I learned and love about the military is that your fellow Soldiers become your extended family. Sometimes, we would hang in Seoul and shop the local markets, sometimes we would take the train or the bus to other military camps in Korea. The shopping was amazing, I could purchase Nike and Coach for the low because it was made in Korea. Designer bags, custom comforters and cozy blankets along with tailor made clothing. I was in a shopping mecca and loving it. I was able to interact with the local citizens, take the train and the bus to various locations and enjoy the local cuisine. I quickly noticed that most of the fruits that I had known to be small here in the states like apples, oranges and lemons were much larger over there and our larger fruits, watermelon for example, was small over there. This was a bit strange but no big deal. The Koreans also had a dish that smelled horrible, but everyone seemed to love to eat it, kimchi. I could never get beyond the whole fermenting process and the smell to eat it. The smell of garlic was in the air as in the Korean culture they cook with it heavily and the smell often came out of their pores. However, they lived long healthy lives.

This is something we should probably look into here in the states instead of msg and sodium. With the exception of initially arriving and getting settled, I didn't really feel lonely or homesick. I wasn't able to make it through my entire tour in Korea, I got sick shortly after arriving. I was tired all the time and couldn't find it in me to get up and make it to the physical fitness formations without getting light-headed and dizzy or vomiting uncontrollably. I stopped reporting for duty on time and thank God I had leadership that were actual leaders. They quickly came to see about me, to talk me through my emotions instead of being so quick to recommend punishment and disciplinary actions. They drove me to the base hospital to get checked out. I wasn't prepared for the life-altering news that I was about to receive. The military providers advised me that I was pregnant and the risk was great to deliver a baby in the Korea economy. I was flooded with emotions. I had just arrived at my first official duty station and I didn't want to disappoint my family with my news. I worried myself sicker than the morning sickness was already making me feel. I remember telling my Squad Leader how afraid I was to tell my mother that I was pregnant and her advising me that I wasn't going to be able to keep this secret for long with the way that it was eating at me. My Squad Leader and Platoon Sergeant became worried and encouraged me to call home and talk to my mom as pregnancy is a very significant milestone in life and in order or to get through it without unforeseen challenges, its essential to avoid stressful situations. They wanted me to have the support of my family. My leadership informed me that I wouldn't be able to complete my tour as it wasn't safe so I would be sent back stateside prior to the birth of my child. I stayed in Korea for five months out of my assigned twelve-month tour. I had to travel before I hit six months as the doctor said anything later would be unsafe. As my return stateside drew nearer, I made that dreaded call home to my mom. We talked about everything on the phone that day. Lord, that was the longest call ever. I felt like I was walking the Green Mile. I made sure to tell her that my best friend had gotten pregnant. I hope y'all caught that.

My mom eventually asked me if I was pregnant and it was like opening the floodgates. Do you remember when your parents would spank you and sometimes when that belt hit your butt your mouth would open to cry but there was a pause and the words wouldn't come right away? That's how I felt, I was so hurt and disappointed in myself and couldn't bear the idea of disappointing my family. I cried so hard the words just wouldn't come. My mom was very understanding. She spoke very softly and told me that everything would be okay. She said' "Baby I'm happy for you if you are happy." Finally, I had a voice. I sobbed, "I'm not happy!" "What am I going to do with a baby?"

At such a young and impressionable age, away from home trying to chart my own way through this thing called life. I was nowhere near prepared for parenthood. Little did I know at the time, that's a part of life. Many people find themselves in that very situation every single day. If I hadn't had mentally and spiritually grounded individuals around me, my circumstances could have been very different. In a day and age where it's easier to abort a baby instead of facing the responsibility of owning your actions and raising your children, I could have been laid up in some off-brand clinic out of my own guilt and shame. Don't get me wrong, I'm not judging abortion, there are circumstances where it could be an option. However, I don't see it fitting in my circumstances at that time. Proverbs 19:20 KJV says to listen to advice and accept instruction, that you may gain wisdom in the future. Many are the plans in the mind of man, but it is the purpose of the Lord that will stand.

To all the young Soldiers and young ladies coming behind me, know that you don't have to have it figured out. It's okay to make mistakes, that's how you learn. Give yourself grace to grow from your mistakes, keep God at the head of your life and He will order your steps by sending the right people at the right time, if only you humble yourself to have an ear to hear and a heart to receive. You will know wise counsel when you hear, you will feel it inside you.

I left Korea and was stationed out of Ft. Stewart, GA. The Third Infantry Division, I was lucky enough to go work at Hunter Army Airfield. This was a blessing as well as at Ft. Stewart the environment was very rural and most of the units were primarily men in Infantry or Armor units. There was absolutely nothing to do in Hinesville. It was truly a town that without the Army base I don't think would have been a town at all. Savannah reminded me a little more of home. There was a mall, restaurants, more housing options and a college. Upon arrival, I reached out to Ron and let him know that I was back in the United States. I also shared the news of our unborn child. He was upset that I hadn't kept contact with him while I was in Korea as promised or at least that's what he said. I had only written him once or twice during the previous five months, true enough however I don't know who he thought he was playing with. One minute I'd talk to him and he was so in love, saying he was coming to Georgia to visit and wanted to maintain a relationship. I didn't have a car yet so I didn't go to visit him and he didn't come to Savannah. With my hormones raging and figuring out that Ron was a liar, it wasn't uncommon to find me outside on the phone cursing out my baby daddy. I didn't care that I was loud or who may have overheard, I didn't make the baby alone and Ron wasn't going to come at me sideways with his lying. I eventually found out not only was the other girl pregnant our babies were a month apart. I was only at Ft. Stewart for about three weeks before relocating to Hunter Army Airfield (Savannah, GA). I wound up getting a townhouse off post. This was my first official place and I was so excited to be in my own place and expecting a baby boy! I met some pretty cool guys at reception. Danny is one that I met at reception, him and Armen. All three of us became friends and they always looked out for me. They thought it was hilarious to find me outside on the payphone not caring who walked by cursing out Ron at any point throughout the day. Danny told me that it turned him on, and I was way too sexy to be worried about that loser. He would drive to Savannah to make sure that I was okay and didn't need anything. Sometimes I didn't even have to ask.

I got my first car after a couple of weeks of being in Savannah. It was an eighty-nine Honda Accord, it wasn't brand new, but it was new to me. It had a sunroof, spoiler and cd player that I could play my 2-Pac, Ginuwine, Goodie Mob and Lil Kim cd's on. Oh, I can't forget about Silk, LSG, Master P, Mystical and my girl Mia X. Music was much different then. I went home for a month before reporting to Ft. Stewart so by the time I arrived I was in my seventh month. I had been in Savannah and snuggled in my apartment for about three months when I went into labor. I didn't know what was going on, my stomach hurt and I felt constipated. I kept trying to use the bathroom but nothing was happening. My mom, stepdad and sisters were on the road to come spend the weekend with me. I called to talk with Grandma and she asked how far away my mom was. I told her a few hours out and she told me that she didn't think that I was constipated and to relax and make sure that I had everything that I wanted to take to the hospital ready. Grandma was right again, my mom arrived just in time to head to the hospital and see witness the birth of her first grandchild. Ron didn't show for the delivery; therefore my son has my last name instead of his dad's. It's probably better that way, Whyte sounds so much better than Leach. I named my baby boy Darius, he was perfect. Bright eyed, head full of hair, his dad's complexion and the sweetest baby ever. I was in love. I had no idea how much this gift from God would change my life. He changed all of our lives. My mom and stepdad spoiled him more than I did. This was the coolest kid ever; he'd sit in his car seat and move his little head and feet to the music. Much more laid back than his who was from zero to a hundred real quick. I left Darius at home with my mom for a few months until I could find childcare in Savannah and to let him get a little older before going to daycare.

I worked with some amazing people. We worked hard, we partied hard and always had each other's back. This was my family away from my family. Although we believed in having a good time, we were still Soldiers. In the military, you still have to be at your place of duty on time with no exceptions. Well, of course emergencies will arise, but you know what I mean. My friend Corinne introduced me to her babysitter, our babies were close in age so, our friendship was a God send. Corinne, Mallory Santasha, and Saundra helped me adjust to motherhood. These ladies were great, we were the workers of the 260th Quartermaster Battalion S-1 along with Tonya and Frances and Denise. I was able to go back and get my baby and get him in daycare. Corinne and I often had playdates with the kids. I frequently had to take my son home because my unit was always training for a mission or having to deploy for various missions. After a few times of taking him back and forth, I just left him home with my mom and sisters for greater stability.

After all the drama with Ron, I didn't want a nice-looking guy to date. I wanted someone that would be faithful, someone that would love me and my son. Isn't it crazy when what you need is right in front of you, but you skip right over it for something else? Danny would have been the perfect guy, but I simply saw him as a friend. I told you hindsight is 20/20. I met Jack, definitely not the cutest, not the tallest and not my norm at all. However, he was nice. He wasn't the cutest, but that was exactly what I wanted, I thought that he'd be faithful. That couldn't have been furthest from the truth. We had a nice relationship until I spotted another girl driving his car and found out that he had been staying with her. I couldn't believe he cheated. Me and my girls went to where he had been staying with the other girl and her family. I walked right up and knocked on the door. I don't know how many people lived in that apartment, but at least four people came to the door before she appeared. She was pretty, lol she was probably thinking the same thing I did. I dated him because I didn't think anyone else would want to. I told her that I had no issues with her but I wanted him to come to the door. My girls and I were ready to beat his ass and destroy that precious car of his too! We dressed in all black, leaving nothing but our eyes out. We had spray paint, can openers, a funnel and some sugar to show his car some special attention too. Someone called the police before we could really get going and we had to leave.

Jack and I didn't get to fight that night, but it was coming. I found out yet again that I was pregnant and so was she. My family doesn't believe in abortion, and against my own beliefs I refused to have another child with a man that wasn't going to be around. I didn't tell my family this time around. I wasn't going to disappoint them; I could barely deal with the depression and disappointment in myself. Y'all already know how I feel about abortions. I knew it was wrong. I wasn't forced, it was consensual sex and out of it, a child had been conceived. Nonetheless, I sought counsel from no one. I wasn't about to have another child with an absentee father. Lord have mercy! When you can't see beyond your own ego and selfish needs. I made Jack drive me to Jacksonville to get the abortion to avoid running into anyone that we may have known. I hated him for lying and cheating and I hated him for not trying to stop me from aborting our baby. I felt that his willingness to take me to the clinic confirmed that he wouldn't be there for me and a baby and there was no way I was going to go through this alone again so soon. Darius was only two years old.

2 Chronicles 7:14 KJV says, *"If my people who are called by my name will humble themselves, pray, seek my face and turn from their wicked ways, then I will hear from heaven and I will forgive their sins and heal their land."*

I had to deploy to Texas a week after the abortion and wound up really ill with an infection shortly after getting there. I didn't tell anyone what I had done, I decided that I would take this to the grave. I didn't tell my healthcare professionals or go back for follow up treatment. I left for deployment like nothing happened. I had to go to the hospital and wound up with quarters for the infection. Had I been open and upfront with my leadership, I wouldn't have been on that deployment and I could have taken better care of myself. Had I prayed on the situation before reacting to my emotions, I wouldn't have been in that mess to begin with. Is it just me or does anyone find that old hymnals learned as a child began to have meaning in your life? "Oh what needless pain we bear, all because we do not carry everything to God in prayer." They didn't apply when we learned them because we lacked experience to relate, but as my Grandma would say, "Just keep on living." Needless to say, I promised God that if He got me through that debacle, I would never do it again. To this day, I've been true to my word. I dumped Jack like a hot potato and I started dating his friend. Tall, light-skinned, beautiful jet-black hair and that smile. He was arrogant as was I. Initially, we argued like no one's business over everything before we finally gave in to our feelings for one another. We had two mutual friends that were dating and often times this put us in one another's company whether we liked it or not. One day he asked me what I would do if he kissed me, I told him to kiss me and find out. Who knew, two people that had been hurt from past relationships became absorbed in themselves, and did I tell you he was Jack's friend? We hit it off and had a beautiful relationship for years.

In the beginning Jack darn near lost his mind. He began following me. He would ride by Tony's place and leave notes on my car. One night, Tony and I were at my place and he saw someone in the window. It was Jack. "Look fool, you made your choice and so have I now take your busted ass on back to ya chick in the hood with all them damn people in that little bitty apartment!" "Tony is more of a man than you could ever be, I wish I had met him first!" I slammed my door and went back to Tony. If Jack didn't know before, he knew then that I was happy with his friend. One day, Jack waited for Tony to leave and walked in the door behind him. When I heard the door, I thought Tony had forgotten something. "Babe what did you forget?" When he didn't answer I turned around and was startled to see Jack standing in my living room. "I miss you" , he said. He tried to kiss me and I pushed him away. "Get out of my apartment!" "Are you crazy?" I told him that he had to get out. He slapped the crap out of me! I couldn't believe that he had put his hands on me. Was he just going to come in and force himself on me and beat me up because I rejected him? I thought about all the years that I watched my mother endure abuse when my sister's dad would come in the house in a drunken rage. I grew up watching and listening to my mother take beatings from a man. There was no way I was going to let someone hurt me like that. I looked up and saw a glade air freshener can on my speaker, I grabbed that can and beat the hell out of Reggie until he got off me and let me go. I then grabbed my keys and took off out the door to my car headed to the military police station. He followed me to tell his side of the story as well. We were both charged with a domestic incident due to the injuries that he had in his head from that glade can. He may have been crazy for real to follow me around town leaving notes on my car and then to come in and try to force himself on me. I later discovered that he cut the seat out of all my lingerie. Despite Jack's efforts, it only strengthened my relationship with Tony.

To all the Soldiers behind me and women in general, domestic violence is not okay. Sexual Assault is not okay. Breaking and entering into someone else's home is not okay. Being followed or following someone else around is not okay. We have to recognize the warning signs of unhealthy relationships and leave or get help before someone gets hurt. No woman or man should endure physical or mental abuse at any level.

I eventually left active duty to return home and continue the military as a reservist. When I left, I was filled with love, memories and more family than I'd left home with a few years prior. Words can't explain the comradery that I experienced. Great leaders and teachers, support and fellowship. We worked together, trained together, partied together and worshipped together. However, something was missing. I missed my son, I wanted to be full-time in his life. Leaving Active Army I sacrificed my career to allow me to spend more time with him. Life as a Reserve Soldier was completely different than what I knew of active duty. We drilled once a month, usually a ton of sitting around not getting much of anything done. The family atmosphere was lacking, everyone seemed to look out for themselves in the beginning. I regretted joining the reserves initially. I stopped going to drill and saw the Army Reserves as a joke. There weren't any consequences and we weren't doing anything anyhow. I vowed that when I got into a leadership position, things would change, until then I just went through the motions. My reserve unit came down on deployment orders to go to Bosnia. I felt there's no way I'm going overseas with these rejects that don't wear their uniforms proudly, they don't show up for work or show any interest about the Soldiers in the unit. I guess deployment makes people respond differently. The leaders shook off their lackadaisical approach and began to take training seriously and they actually began to become accountable for themselves and others. I had a few friends leave active duty and get assigned to the same unit, which made me want to attend more frequently as well. One day, my Supply Sergeant pulled me to the side to talk to me and find out why I had been so quiet or nonexistent in the unit. I shared with him my thoughts of the unit and he explained the feelings that I had, most Soldiers that have served in active component to the reserves had felt the same way. There were also many Soldiers in the unit that had never been active duty but they were good people. He told me to just give them a chance. This is my advice to any Soldier leaving active military transitioning into the Reserves.

The same way God gives us grace for our shortfalls in life, it's our duty to give grace to others along the way.

On my initial enlistment contract and while serving in the Army Reserves, I met my husband and we had two children. We weren't married at the time. In fact, he was still married when we met. That's another book for another day. My husband blessed me with our daughter. Tiendra, my gorgeous baby girl. She was perfect with a head full of hair and very healthy. I decided not to renew my contract after returning from Bosnia and giving birth to our daughter. I took a break from military service and enjoyed being a mom. There were so many things that I regretted missing with my oldest that I didn't want to miss a beat with my baby girl. While we were in Bosnia, 9/11 took place back here in the states. Upon my return from Bosnia, I got to enjoy motherhood and my child's father went back to training to prepare for deployment to Iraq. The distance was rough, and he missed out on experiencing our daughter beginning to grow. Upon his return and just before his next deployment, I got pregnant with our son. Tyree, the youngest and the smallest baby that I had given birth to. Tyree was my ball of energy, destined to keep me on my toes. Sounds like the life of an Army wife. Being in a relationship with a Soldier isn't for the faint of heart. Military men and women risk their lives to provide the American way of life for every citizen of the United States. In countries riddled with war, there are huge disparities like clean water, safe and hazard free housing conditions, access to healthcare the ability to get up and go where you want when you want. These are things often taken for granted until you're in an environment that doesn't have it. This is something that I'm forever grateful to my service to this country for. I was allowed to see life through the lives of citizens in other countries, to pray with them, to eat with them and to cry for them, when I thought of how blessed we were stateside.

I decided to go back and enlist in the Army Reserves after a four-year break in service. I signed a new contract with the Army Reserves and my new assignment was a lot like my first reserve assignment. Only this time I had three children and my focus was different. My priority was raising my babies and being able to advance my career at the same time. My friend and Retention NCO took me upstairs to my new command. For the first time ever, I saw an entire leadership chain that looked like me. They were predominantly African American. Don't get me wrong, I love all races. However, I had never been in a unit where the leadership was predominantly black men and women. I don't care what your race is as a woman or a man, when you see people that look like you excel in leadership and rise to the forefront of their careers, that's something to feel good about. You should celebrate the work of others and strive for excellence as well, so that when the time comes you will know what it is to lead and how to lead others effectively.

However, at that time, I was still young and very inexperienced in the upper echelons of leadership in the military. I didn't realize the weight that these individuals carried. For the first time in my military history I witnessed and experienced blatant racism, gender bias and hostile workplace environment. I learned that being black and in leadership, meant you were judged much more harshly than your Caucasian and Hispanic counterparts and God forbid, don't be a black woman! Every action, every word, and every thought seems to be under a microscope. Yes, I'm going to explain. I had a firm Executive Officer who took no shortcuts. She accepted me into the unit. She counseled me and molded me into a true Soldier, one that was capable of leading. She showed me that when you feel you've done your best, go back and look at it again, check for errors and omissions.

Many individuals despised such firmness, but I not only welcomed it, I truly appreciated it. I knew that she didn't have to take time in explaining the details, molding and developing us. It hurt me to my heart to see that even your own people will despise your works, no matter how good you are. Your works simply aren't enough because of your gender. My Executive Officer sat me down and showed me how all of my wasted time in the military was just that, wasted time and it wouldn't count towards my retirement. You see, I didn't know that in the Reserves you had to attend battle assembly weekend and your two-week annual training or get an excused absence in order for your years to count towards your retirement. She told me to never give anyone power over myself or my future. I will forever love and respect her for that and the life she exemplified. She spoke to me and my fellow Soldiers. Working underneath her leadership, I worked in the S-1 and learned my job with great detail. Major Smith and my Noncommissioned Officer-In-Charge SFC Williams, were very instrumental in molding me into a career-oriented individual that would give grace for a very promising future. I competed for a civilian job as a Unit Administrator and was selected for the position. However, there were some leaders who felt that my younger, Hispanic colleague should have gotten the job. They even contested the ranking order to see if I was truly qualified. Little did I know, that would be the first of a long list of battles faced within this command.

I held the job of Unit Administrator for about nine months. During those nine months, I experienced pure hell. No matter how good of a job I did, it was never good enough. You see, as a Unit Administrator my leadership chain changed. I had to work for and with the very people that didn't consider me qualified enough, or light enough if you get my drift for the position. None-the-less, I ran the reports and pushed them out to the Commander, First Sergeant and Platoon as I should have. I requested feedback and gave suspense dates for information to be turned back in. There was little to no compliance. This negatively affected the timeliness of Soldiers pay, evaluations and awards. I would refer back to my leadership chain on the Soldier side for assistance and intervention. I had never in my military career received such blatant disrespect and disregard in a professional setting. I had to find a way to break through this barrier. I did, instead of relying on leadership as a frontline of communication. I began communicating directly with the Soldiers that may have had personnel actions needed to be processed and I would courtesy copy the leadership in on the correspondence. This resolved many issues but there were a chosen few.

No matter how much I gave, no matter how hard I worked, no matter how early I came or how late I stayed they always found a way to have something to complain about. Even if it meant that they would miss a deadline or make false accusations, they were hell bent trying to find a way to discredit me or the work that I did. Thankfully, I worked very closely with the S-1 and they were aware of the nonsense. Major Smith pulled me into her office one day and had a heart-to-heart conversation with me. She asked me, "How many African-American females are there in the intelligence field in the Army Reserves?" I had never paid it any attention until that time. I never really had to. She was one of a chosen few. After our conversation, I saw my command differently. I realized that while the S-1 leadership was predominantly black men and women, my initial amazement was correct, that certainly wasn't the norm of most commands.

This Command was special in it was made up of Soldiers that affected the many secrets that our military hold near and dear regarding upcoming missions states-side and abroad, mission details and intelligence information and surveillance for those missions. Many of the Soldiers in this detachment were lawyers, judges, politicians and law enforcement in their civilian capacity. One would have thought this would have been a great thing, however these same individuals felt that the rest of us were the help and didn't deserve to be in leadership over them. The tension in the air was so thick you could cut it with a knife between the S-1 staff and these legal, intelligence forces. I had walked into an all-out war between the two detachments. Major Smith relocated to another duty station, a few others retired and changed duty stations and all hell broke loose. There was no one left to keep things in a professional working relationship anymore.

You see Major Smith outranked most of them in rank and by her position. They may not have liked it but there was nothing they could do about it. Crazy thing is....those weren't the only opposing forces that she had to contend with. Many of the African American men in leadership positions disliked her as well and wanted her gone. While she was the glue that held everything together, when she left those African American males turned a blind eye to the blatant racism, gender bias and hostile work environment that we were in. I believe that I may have lasted about three to four months after her departure.

One week in September 2009, we had several Soldiers in the office performing their annual training by helping with personnel and administrative actions. One Soldier in particular, SGT Whyte left to go grab a bite to eat and was involved in a car accident. I filled out an incident report and gave it to the Commander to complete his portion, so that we could process it to ensure that the Soldier's care was covered. The Commander indicated that the Soldier was not on Active Duty at the time of the accident. Me, always trying to walk in the spirit of integrity and taking care of Soldiers figured that it was a mistake. I made the correction on the form to indicate that the Soldier was in fact in an active capacity at the time the accident occurred. I advised him of the change and gave it to him to initial the corrections so that I could upload the documents for processing. Nothing could have prepared me for what came next. The Commander, a Caucasian male had the highest ranking African American female on duty Sergeant Major Phyllis to come get me and escort me to his office. He sat me down and advised me that I was fired! He couldn't fire me from my Soldier enlistment contract, so he stated that I was fired from the Unit Administrator position. How could this be? I was on annual training as well, for my non-military folks out there I wasn't serving in the capacity upon which he was firing me which was a clear violation on top of the fact that he lied and stated that the Soldier was on Active Duty and that I falsified the document by changing his response. I was mad as hell, but I didn't break. "Are you sure that you want to fire me from my civilian job while I'm in uniform drilling this weekend?" I told him that what he was doing was wrong. I pointed out the fact that he couldn't punish me in my civilian role while I was serving in my military role as the two roles aren't to be intertwined. "Sir with all due respect, I assumed that you made a mistake on the form as the Soldier was on annual training orders at the time of the accident." Technically, I didn't falsify the document, you did". "I assumed that your entry was in error and made the correction, brought it back to you to initial the change." He negated everything that said and advised. "You're still fired. Although you're fired from your civilian job, I fully expect you to continue your Soldier obligations and be at drill as required." "Are my instructions clear?" He asked and dismissed me from the meeting. I already had an open Equal Employment Opportunity complaint against my Chain of Command for racial and gender bias and hostile work environment. I called my attorney to advise him of the firing. He told me not to worry and that he'd take it from there. "Hahaha" I laughed, I cried and I cursed in utter disbelief that this could happen. My lawyer told me that this was reprisal and that he would file the necessary paperwork. My Retention NCO and friend transferred me to another unit immediately to continue drilling as a Soldier as it was apparent that nothing good would come out of serving under this new Commander.

The lawsuit went on for years. However, not only did I win the case I was reinstated with promotion and relocated all expenses paid. During the time off, my car was repossessed, there were times that I didn't know how I would pay the bills or put food on the table. *Did you hear me say that the reinstatement came with promotion ...God will give you beauty for ashes if you just hold on.* On judgment day those legal intellectuals and "leaders" of our elite forces lied one after the other during our mediation. The attorney for the military just dropped his head in utter disbelief. I shook my head in amazement thinking, if they were going to lie, I would have thought that they would have at least gotten together to get their stories straight.

Everyone had to tell their name, race, ethnicity and answer whether or not I did my job and how well I did my job. One after the other the answer ruled in my favor. The mediator asked, ``What's the issue if she performed her tasks above what was required?" Not one of them could say. I received compensation for my lost wages and attorney's fees and continued my career without any further setback or interruption.

The best moment of all came a few years later when I was stationed in the exact same building as the unit that had created so many emotional scars. This time I worked downstairs with a Military Police unit. I came in the building and ran into one of those good ole boy individuals that came to the unit with a mission to whiten up the unit after Major Smith pcs'd. "Ha-ha," he looked like he had seen a ghost. "I'm surprised to see you still around." That's what he said when he saw me. I know what you're thinking, the nerve of him! That surely was my thought as well. However, I looked at him with a smile on my face and said, "I was reinstated to a Supervisory Unit Administrator position where I ran a company of over three hundred Soldiers and three civilians. The Department of Defense relocated my family and I all expenses paid to Richmond, Virginia." " I have just relocated back to the area after the retirement of my husband, Command Sergeant Major Anthony Smith and we are making the Tampa Bay area our home." That felt so good. He couldn't say a word, and my response wiped that smug look right off his face.

To all of my fellow Soldiers as sad as it is, racial ethnic hatred exists in the military. Gender, age, ethnic and disability discriminations exists in the military. Sometimes it may seem as though things aren't getting any better or just won't work out. I say to you, don't grow weary in well doing. You shall reap what you sow if you faint not. Show up, be where you are supposed to be when you're supposed to be there. As a Soldier myself, as a spouse to a Soldier and a single parent I believe that I've witnessed quite a bit in my years in service. I've survived domestic violence twice, I'm a sexual assault survivor, I survived racial ethnic, gender hatred and hostile work environment. I've been accused and ethnic hatred. Not only have I experienced these things, I studied them. I went to school to learn how to help other Soldiers avoid them and handle them if faced with any of these challenges. Not only have I served as an Administrative Assistant later becoming a Human Resource Specialist, I became a Unit Victim Advocate to stand against Sexual Assault and Sexual Harassment, I became an Equal Opportunity Leader to raise awareness of cultural diversity and bias so that no one would have to deal with that in our ranks. I stand as a voice to those that may feel as if they have no voice. I am here to tell you that you will win! It doesn't matter your past, it doesn't matter how messed up you may think you are, sis you win in the end if you just keep the faith. Show up, exceed expectations when performing your tasks and drills. Get to know the policies and regulations, education truly is the key to fighting the battles that you may encounter. Lastly, in the words of our former First Lady Michelle Obama, "When they go low, we go high."

Victor In This Battle

CHAUNDRA NICOLE GORE

I raised my hand Oct 18, 1999 to be apart of one of the best organizations on the earth, the United States Army Reserve. I know I was destined to lead after spending four years in the Junior Reserve Officer Training Program in high school. I could hear the cadences being played in my mind, "shoot, move, and communicate." There I was in basic training at Fort Jackson, South Carolina beginning a new journey that would transform me from civilian to Soldier. The air I breathed was different. I could feel the vibration of order, respect, duty, honor, selfless service, personal courage, and leadership every time I took a step. The formations made me feel as if I had order and was organized for the first time in years. The sound of a synchronized voice sounding off, made my heart tremble with victory. I loved it, enjoyed every moment of my journey so far.

Roaring with excitement, I exited the bus in front of the in-processing facility and all I could hear was, "*Get off the bus privates, get your bags and run, if you packed it, you carry it, lets go NOW!*" Drill sergeants screaming at us to run with all of our stuff? I didn't practice that. I practiced military bearing, drill and ceremony, and how to render proper courtesies. What we got right off the bus was unexpected. After becoming acquainted with the drill sergeants, I knew I was up for the challenge. I had to condition my mind to push hard and stay motivated to get to the finish line.

Nine weeks of physical fitness, battle drills, marksmanship, and constant soldiering transformed me into a dedicated servant to my country. I embodied the seven Army values and how to lead by example by setting the example. I was so fired up about being a Soldier that I pushed through every hurdle that came my way. I simply shut my mouth, kept my head up and became the Soldier of the cycle. I fought hard and persisted to be the best, by working harder than I could ever imagine and believing in myself and my abilities. Every time I felt pain, I told myself that it was weakness leaving the body.

This helped propel me forward through the pain to continue to work hard and set the example for others around me. I helped others by pushing them to fight through their pain, anguish, loneliness, and sadness. I told some of my fellow comrades *"pain is just weakness leaving the body"* because that is what I was taught. I put the mental picture of my mom in front of me on every run, because I was running for her. I knew in my mind I had to get back to my mother, but I wanted to go back with purpose and make a difference as a Soldier, so I couldn't give up on the process. Oftentimes when things get tough, we want to throw the towel in and give up, but God gave me the strength and ability to *push* hard and that is exactly what I did, for myself and everyone I came in contact with, while I was in training. I had a great team of drills that taught me everything I know.

No one prepared me for nothing else, but being a Soldier. I never knew there was a dark underworld of the military and that was sex, lust, fornication and adultery. When I raised my hand, I never pictured myself as a sex object, a piece of meat or a fling, but as I navigated the training environment, I was approached several times for sex, a night out, a "quicky." I made it to Advanced Individual Training (AIT) and I finally gave into my on flesh and I had sex. Imagine a bunch of people being put together from all over the world and many having left their significant other. How does the hormones of the body adapt to that drastic change? From my perspective, in the military sometimes you meet someone else and take care of your needs or wait until you are done with training. This is where your inner strength comes into play. We fight with our flesh day in and day out. I didn't really know about this in spiritual terms back then.

Everyone was away from home, in their flesh and ready to mingle. It was almost as if it was the culture of the training environment and it didn't seem wrong. It seemed as if you had to have sex in order to get your needs met, or to please someone else. Hell, if you saw someone that looked good you wanted to get with them because you have been trapped in the training environment with people you don't even know and who you want back at home isn't available, so what do you do? Now that I am at a different place in my life, I see it clearly for what it was back then. Leaving the base on a pass and meeting someone that cleaned up well, because you know all you ever saw them in was a uniform. When the uniforms came off and everyone put on their best, suddenly your sex drive kicked into high gear and you either looking at someone like they are a piece of meat or they are looking at you as a piece of meat. I had a crew that I drew close to and we all hung out together. I didn't know God then like I know Him now. I made some decisions back then to have sex to calm my sex drive without consulting the Lord. I was young and enjoying life. Living in the moment, progressing in life and trying to make a difference was difficult. So many of us sisters in arms fell in where we thought we belonged to pass the time. I just really wanted love, and to be held by somebody after all this hard training I had been through.

As I reflect on my time in training, I think about all the days I wanted to go home, but every time I thought about home, I was only really missing my mom and family. The streets were calling, but it wasn't enough to make me quit being a Soldier and doing something different for my life. I have always wanted to make a dent with my dash and if that meant sacrificing my time, I was all for it. I knew that in the end I would have a career that I was passionate about. I absolutely loved being a Soldier and motivating others seemed so natural for me. I could do it blindfolded and with my hands tied behind my back, that's how passionate I was from the very start.

I believed my past sexual abuse opened the door for my promiscuity in training and in my life period. I craved it and wanted it, but never did I think someone would try and take it from me. That happened to me one night while out drinking on the weekend, someone tried me and I had to fight him off. My crew got a hotel room and we had food and drinks. We were playing cards and one of the men lost the game and he proceeded to get up and start dancing and joking. The other two said they were going to step outside for a minute and talk. I got up to go to the bathroom and I was grabbed by my arm and was slung down on the bed. At first, I thought it was a playful manner, but when I saw the aggression on his face, it felt really real to me at that point. I did everything I could to fight him off, bit him, scratched him and even kicked him in the balls. He thought I wanted it because I was drinking with him and a few others, but I didn't. I didn't want him, I wanted his friend if the truth be told. When he figured out that I had some, "hood" in me, he backed off because I was about to knock him upside his head with a closet pole. I saw the closet pole in the distance and I knew, if I could just get a loose I would crack his ass with it.

Guess what that blow to his balls allowed me to break free and I grabbed that pole, he started screaming then, "don't hit me, don't hit me girl, you are crazy". I said, "oh, you was trying to take it huh, I will show you". I saw strength and power rise up in me, at the same time as anger. I couldn't believe it, that night changed my entire perspective on training. I also blamed myself for being in a position to allow that to happen. I couldn't believe the level of escalation, but I was young and in my flesh of course and drinking on top of that. I can honestly say that after that ordeal was over, I was very sober. I never said anything because of the position in which I placed myself. I knew better and as training ended, I knew I would be heading back home anyway, so I saw no need to stir up a big mess. This was clearly sexual assault, but I didn't report it and I should have. I thought it was cool for me to play it safe and just carry on with my life.

When the other two returned they asked where my assailant went and I told them what happened and they were in shock. The male comrade said, "are you sure, he really likes you and I don't think he would try nothing like that". I said to him, "yes he really got aggressive with and wanted to take the pussy, ask him what happened and take a good look at the pain he is in". He said, "I will, as a matter of fact, let me track him down now because we have to go back on base together". My female comrade and I stayed at the room a little while longer talking through what happened that night and then we ordered more food and just watched a movie until the next day we then returned to base. I tried my best to bury everything that happened to me over the weekend and I was successful in doing so, I thought. I never knew it would turn me into a mean and angry woman moving forward, but it did.

Back then, no one was really open to talking about their sexual abuse or harassment like in today's society. You kept your mouth shut back then and carried on with your day. The hurt, shame, and pain was buried and carried on with you for the rest of your life or until you decided to talk about it and write your story like I am doing in this anthology. A common question many abuse victims ask themselves is, will anyone believe me? I didn't have that fear. I thought it would lead to unwanted drama or take away from where I was trying to go in life, so I buried it. I didn't want to lose sight of my vision, journey, and my destiny as a Soldier. We were not encouraged to report like they are now. I don't even remember hearing about S.H.A.R.P. when I was in training.

Once I became a Sexual Harassment Assault Response and Prevention Victim Advocate (SHARP), the way I felt about my own situation resurfaced. I started to talk about it more, and shared my experience. I realized that I buried a real incident and carried it throughout my life and thought that was okay. In actuality it wasn't. I sought help for my very own sexual trauma and felt so much better. 12 years later, I sought help for what I went through. It was very beneficial for me and it actually helped me to be a better victim advocate. I absolutely love what I do and had I not been through sexual abuse and assault/harassment, I would not be able to show up big for other men and women.

God allows things to happen to us so that He can get the glory. We don't realize it when we go through things, all we say is why me Lord? He doesn't give us anymore than we can handle. If it's on us, God will see us through it. He believes that we have the ability to grow through whatever is placed in our path. I have learned to lean on God and not my own understanding, like I did in the past. I now use my voice to encourage, motivate and inspire other men and women to fight past the pain so they can heal and be someone else's Moses. God always has a way to turn our mess into a message for others. Some people think that the trials and tribulations they face is for them, but it is actually for others to learn, understand and grow through what they are going through. We have the ability to save lives and help others if we just tell our story. If you never tell it, then no one can hear it. There is always someone, somewhere that is waiting on your outcome so they can make a better choice for themselves.

As we have most recently seen in the news, sexual assault allegations and charges are coming out left and right. It is more acceptable these days for people to come forward and make a statement. Making a false claim makes it bad for people that have a real claim to be trusted and believed. It is very important for each case to be investigated to the fullest extent of the law and then a judgement rendered appropriately. In the Army, we have an office that is designed to appropriately handle all sexual assault and harassment cases. This office has increased in stability and effort over time. The campaigns for SHARP have changed year after year, in an effort to remain relevant and ready to be more open to receive cases, but the overall message remains the same. Any SHARP victim's advocate or office operating as such, is open and committed to providing the support you need, when you need it.

In 2018, the Army started a SHARP campaign called, "Not in Our Army," this allowed units from all over the world to join in and make a bold statement that sexual assault and harassment would not be tolerated in their unit, squad, or platoon. This is a great campaign that continues to flourish throughout the units nationwide and overseas. I participated in making a video that was designed to boost morale as well as bring awareness. The Army has Sexual Assault Response Coordinators and Victim Advocates trained to receive restricted and unrestricted reports.

The SARC serves as a single point of contact to coordinate victim care. The Victim Advocate provides support and care to the victim, non-clinical information, unit transfer options, reporting options, and procedures. There's a huge difference between restricted and unrestricted reporting. Unrestricted reporting you can receive medical treatment, counseling, advice, and representation by a Special Victim Counsel, SARC and VA assistance, and an official investigation. The restricted reporting is for those that want to remain confidential without initiating an investigation, they can contact the SARC, VA, or healthcare provider. Those that choose the restricted reporting will still be able to receive assistance, it just does not initiate an investigation.

Restricted reporting has limitations which must be disclosed to the victim such as: the assailant remains unpunished, no military protective order issued, there may be continued contact with your assailant, evidence may be lost, you won't be able to discuss the case, and you will be ineligible for a transfer. However, you can always change to unrestricted if you so desire. The Safe Helpline supports Sexual assault for the DOD community, you can reach them at safehelpline.org or 877-995-5247.

During my tenure as an active victim's advocate, each victim I came in contact with was afraid of retaliation, being made fun of, ridiculed by the assailant or anyone who they thought may know what is going on if an investigation was opened, and or being transferred away from their support group to another location.

They had mixed feelings about the process and or the care involved. I talked to them all the time to reassure them of the process, take them to where they needed to be, encouraged them to relax and take some time for themselves via yoga, massage therapy, or meditation. I have watched them go from victim to survivor to victor and regain their presence in their own lives. This is very important because you don't want your victim to become suicidal or deeply depressed. I had a duty to make sure they were receiving the necessary care and support they needed.

This was one of my best jobs. It allowed me to serve in an area I knew a lot about because I went through it myself. I didn't get the help and care I gave to them, so I was always trying my best to go above and beyond to make them feel safe and cared for. I continued to show my passion for this cause because I want people to understand that this is so very real and personal to those that go through it. You don't really know the feeling unless it happens to you. I consider myself to be a victor in this sexual assault/harassment/abuse battle. I was a victim, then survivor and now a victor as I advocate for women, men and children. This is my passion to serve and be as effective as I possibly can while I impact, save, and change lives.

It is very important to know that sexual assault and harassment is very real for men, women and children.

The National Sexual Assault Hotline is 1-800-656-HOPE (4763). We must adopt a culture of breaking the silence about a crime and listen to be a solution and not re-victimize others. Know the Facts about SHARP: sexual assault is any form of sexual contact without consent and is normally by force, physical threats or abuse of authority. It is a crime of violence and not passion, it is ultimately about power and dominating the other person. One sexual assault occurs every 2 minutes, which equals 30 victims every hour.

Lastly, I want to encourage everyone to be aware of your surroundings and establish boundaries before you start drinking and try not to be with anyone that you can't trust. Being distracted increases your chances of becoming a victim or target of violence. Open your eyes and ears. Take note of your surroundings when you are out and about. If you know you will be drinking, make sure you establish your ride home and be with a person or people whom you can trust. 90% of acquaintance rapes involve alcohol use. 80% of sexual assaults occur during social activities like dates or parties. 23% of college men have admitted to getting drunk or stoned to engage in sexual intercourse. Most common drugs used during a rape or assault are alcohol, GHB, ketamine, or rohypnol. Data supplied by www.psacorp.com

Through It All, God's Grace Kept Me!

DIANE ADAMS

am so glad God had other plans for me and gave me some direction. Eventually, I did get married but not to my high school boyfriend, thank God! I decided to follow in my dad's footsteps and join the military. He retired Air Force and I went into the Army. I started in the Army Reserve thinking I didn't want to commit completely, and I didn't want to leave home. I also met a guy at the famous USA skating rink when I came home on Christmas break and I wanted to come home and be with him. Looking back now I know that was for the three babies I would soon have. I got pregnant shortly after meeting him. It was so quick my good friend Buffy wasn't sure if she wanted to congratulate me or feel sorry for me. It didn't matter at that point because baby number one was cooking in my belly. It was important that I not be a "statistic", you know young, black unwed mother. My aunt had always told me "Diane, whatever you do, keep all your eggs in one basket", meaning (make the father of my children the same man) so that is what I planned on doing.

I miscarried that first pregnancy. After waiting for my body to heal, we agreed to try for another baby. The next month I was pregnant again. I had my first son, William, on March 21, 1991. He was my ONLY focus. I loved and protected him from everything I could protect him from. His dad didn't seem to want to be bothered with him. He was so mean to him. I remember one day I was washing dishes in the galley style kitchen in our apartment. My son wasn't walking yet so I put him on his blanket and propped him up in the walkway from the dining room to the kitchen, where I could see him and play with him. He was fussing, and it was not bothering me one bit. It was good for him. His dad came in, grabbed a "big gulp" beverage cup (the cup from 7 Eleven), filled it with water and threw it in his face and told him to shut up. He was just 6 months or so and I went crazy! I yelled at him, "what the hell are you doing?" He said, "he needs to shut up". At that moment I embraced William even more. I would never leave him alone with his dad, but I stayed in the marriage for many more years. 2 ½ years later we had another child. I really wanted a girl so I could have a boy and a girl and be done with kids. But God had another plan. Donavyn was born on January 5,1994. He was his dad's baby. He could not do anything wrong. I was so excited to have two boys. They were easy while in their pre-teen years. They were my life but still something was missing; my happiness was missing. I was unhappy in my marriage. I was going through the motions and making everyone close to me happy. Kids were happy and husband was happy. Remember I met and married only because I was pregnant. I don't know why I didn't leave him after having the first miscarriage except to say the kids that came after the miscarriage were meant to be here. We didn't take time to get to know each other before kids and marriage came.

In 1997, I divorced their dad and joined the Army full time. My life changed drastically once I made that decision. The boys lived with their father full time and I was stationed at Fort Hood in Texas. Before leaving Ohio, I was dating again and I remarried knowing it was for the wrong reason. Marrying for children, not wanting to be alone and feeling like no one wanted me were my reasons for getting married. Not once did I think to ask God, is this the man you have for me. Again, the relationship was horrible from the beginning. You know it's bad when NONE of your family shows up for the wedding because they didn't approve of it and they knew better than I. He was abusive and the relationship deteriorated ending in a divorce.

While stationed in Texas I was the executive secretary to the Command Sergeant Major and Colonel. I had the best boss ever, but like I said before the marriage was not good one to be desired. We were in Texas for about a year before my then-husband left and went back to Ohio. I was alone in Texas and felt like I really had no one. Fort Hood was my first active duty station and I didn't have any friends or anyone that I hung out with at this point. I found comfort in doing Physical Training (PT) at dusk just before going to bed. Just when the sun is going down and it wasn't so hot outside, I went for a run. I will be honest, I did just as much walking as running. This evening, it was nice outside. The wind was blowing. It wasn't too hot or sticky out. I ran to the start of the trail and about 10 minutes into my run I see these two guys in the distance. It's getting darker, I decided to head back to the house. These guys were coming toward me. Fear began to rise up inside of me. One of the guys grabbed me and other was saying "get her feet!". They pulled me into the wood line, falling to the ground just as we got far enough off the trail not to be seen. They were strong and smelled so bad! While being held down my hands were tied with shoestring. It was so dark at this point, and I couldn't see what they looked like. I just wanted this horror to be over! They RAPED Me! I had not been at Fort Hood long before I was raped. I PROMISED myself I would never tell anyone. I blamed myself. I shouldn't have been out there anyway! I didn't know what they looked. I REALLY didn't want to be the victim. I gathered myself, hurried back to the house, showered and suppressed the stream of emotions that came with the trauma I had just experienced. My thought was to call my husband and ask him if we could work it out.

Shortly after him moving back home, we got orders to Hawaii and we moved within a few months. I was able to make friends and gaining my footing. Meeting up with my co-workers after work to have drinks and chillin' was my current situation. All was well, except he didn't trust me. I find out later he didn't trust me with my female friends. One in particular because she was gay. The relationship with my husband became verbally and physically abusive. Here I was yet again in a bad situation. This time I was surrounded with friends and my command helped me with so much. I gained the courage to tell my husband I wanted a divorce. He was not in agreement. I confided in my boss who was the Command Sergeant Major and he told my husband he had 30 days to get out of our apartment. Now, let me explain when you live in government housing your command could end up all in your business! This was a good thing for me at the time. I had to find somewhere to stay for 30 days. In my effort to not stay in the barracks, I stayed with friends and in hotels. I had to fight the thoughts that kept crowding my mind saying, "it wasn't that bad, you can go back and make him understand'. But UNDERSTAND WHAT? I not once said "I LOVE YOU" or "The Holy Spirit revealed to me blah blah blah...". I kept telling myself "STAY WITH THE COURSE. GO THROUGH THE PROCESS". After 30 days he was gone, along with everything in the house. Including the food in the refrigerator and cabinets. All he left me was some of my clothes. I did some research and found out he gave away my furniture and he took some things to the pawn shop. I never got any of those things back.

I was, of course still communicating with my ex-husband, the father of my kids, and we reignited talks about getting back together and having another baby. Remember, I had it in my mind to "keep all my eggs in one basket". It made sense to me to try this relationship again. Maybe it would be different this time. Maybe we have matured, and it would work this time. He and the boys moved to Hawaii and we remarried. The marriage still wasn't good, since the only thing that changed was time, we just didn't know that at the time. But I was determined to try.

We have orders to go to Ohio, and I am excited because I was promoted and will have more responsibility at work. Also, I will be at home close to my family. I'm also still concerned about the ability to have this little baby that we are wanting to have. After my youngest sons' birth, I had a tubal ligation. In the reversal procedure only one side was successfully reversed. We were serious about having a baby, but only wanting a girl since we had two boys. After doing much research and trying many Chinese secrets, I finally conceived. You see before leaving Hawaii I had another miscarriage and really wasn't sure if I could or would be able to conceive and carry a baby. At home with family and still in the military, life is going to be alright now, so I thought!

Our daughter was born on February 27, 2004. I felt like all was well, no pain, and it was an easy birth. I had restored communication with my oldest sister, and all my "important" relationships were okay.

On March 3, 2004, while walking down the hall, I had the worst headache of my life. I felt it quickly get worse. The pain felt like needles piercing through my head. I told my husband that I was going to go to Kroger and get some Excedrin. It's the headache medicine, it should work. I cannot find the words to describe the pain, none of the words in the dictionary are good enough. Needless to say, I never made it to the store. We had a bilevel split home, my husband was downstairs with the kids. I was upstairs feeling the worst pain that I had ever felt in my life; it was a consistent piercing for which there was no relief. I had tried laying down, and nothing helped. I walked to the top of the stairs and I turned to call his name, everything went black. One minute I could see and the next I couldn't. My husband called my mother and told her to come get me and take me to the emergency room. I was scared, was my vision was gone? Mom was just about 15 minutes or so away and could take me to the emergency room while he stayed with the kids.

I remember getting to the emergency room and sitting at the triage desk. I couldn't answer any of her questions. However, I did know I had to use the bathroom, so my mom took me into the bathroom, but I don't recall ever coming out. The doctors tell my mother an aneurysm had exploded in my brain. I can only go off of what the transcripts and my family say at this point. I read the hospital transcripts and it spoke of a time when I was yelling "hallelujah" over and over and over again. Doctor's sedated me and performed a 2-hour surgery, after which they told my family that we just have to wait 24 hours to see if what they did, would save my life. The next thing I remember is waking up in ICU with a tube down my throat, unable to communicate. My Pastor, Dr. Forbes, and family were around me. I remember "signaling" for my Aunt to give me something to write with. She did, but I was unable to convey what I was trying to tell her.

The damage from the bleeding in my brain was more significant than I or my family knew. I was in ICU for about a week. I was moved to a regular room and then on to inpatient therapy and progressively to outpatient therapy. While working through inpatient therapy friends and family were there to help me regain what I lost. Stacey, one of my best friends, was a nail tech, came to the hospital to do my nails. My aunt, Annette, was stationed overseas and found a way to reach me during my physical therapy. That had me in tears! My cousin, Sheri, was a nurse at Mount Carmel West hospital, where I was recovering. She would come down and sit with me from time to time. The love from them was exactly what I needed at the time. When I was released and going to outpatient therapy a couple of times a week, I was slowly getting better. I couldn't drive yet, but even riding in the car and seeing the trees go by so fast was causing me anxiety. So, I would lay my seat back so I couldn't see anything. I tell you the anxiety part still happens today. When someone else is driving I often get anxious. Once I was home and trying to learn and work through my new reality, I became depressed. I went from being the breadwinner of my family to not being able to pay bills, read, write, walk without assistance, take care of my ten and thirteen-year old's or take care of this new baby that I FORGOT I birthed. We had just purchased a new home, built from the ground, and a new car. Gradually God started bringing things back to my remembrance.

Because my memory was lost in the process of the aneurysm there were things that I began to slowly remember. Nearly 4 years had lapsed since I had talked to my mother because my husband and mother had an argument. While I was in inpatient therapy. He would not allow my family to come see me or the kids. He had total control over my life.

I was attending Franklin University, before giving birth to my daughter, working on my bachelor's degree in Business Management and Human Resource Management. By God's grace, I went on to finish that degree. The Army medically retired me, meaning my children and I will be set financially. I knew I would not just be able to sit in the house and do nothing. I knew God had much bigger plans for me. I was not sure how that would play out, but I knew it would be something better than what I had going on. I was grateful to not have to worry about money or what I was going to do to make ends meet for me and the kids, but I was still at the mental mercy of my husband. Until God began to bring the details of our marriage back to my remembrance. I remembered I was getting a divorce and I needed to take back control of my life.

I separated from my husband in 2008 and got an apartment with my best friend of 40 years, Karla. Karla was going through a divorce at the same time. We figured, why not get a spot together and this way we could help each other. So, that is what we did. At this point I was being accused of cheating, although he had done that many times in the course of our marriage. He was telling my boys that I was having an affair and I am sure he was telling them many other things that I don't know about. I was not in a position where, mentally, I even cared.

My divorce was final on December 10, 2010 and I was in a custody battle over my daughter. The boys were old enough to decide where they wanted to be. My oldest son decided he wanted to be with me, and my youngest son wanted to be with his dad. What broke my heart was the fact that my daughter did not know me... she wanted to be with her dad. That was a battle that would take me a few years to get through.

I wasn't sure how my disability was going to hold me back or if I would be able to get a job. My memory was horrible, I had a loss of peripheral vision, and some cognitive issues as well. God will give us just what we need to do, exactly what He has called us to do. At this point my disability was not holding me back. I was offered a position at Franklin University as a Student Service Advisor. I loved the position because I worked with military students who were seeking their degree. It allowed me an opportunity to get connected to members of the military again.

In 2010 things started turning around for me. I was sharing living expenses with my mother and getting ready to move to Fayetteville, North Carolina. I had finally met the man God had for me. I met my husband, Chris, on Blackpeoplemeet.com. I promise, two days after creating my profile on the site, he and I began to communicate for hours. He is an Air Force veteran and was working as a contractor in Afghanistan. This was perfect because it would not allow for any physical interaction for some time, and it allowed us to really get to know each other. We met in January 2010, we scheduled and paid for a cruise in February 2010 and met in person around July 2010 (his birth month).

After a year of dating, I moved into his home in Fayetteville North Carolina. I was still dealing with depression and it only got worse when I moved to North

Carolina. I put too much focus on my loss. Chris was not home a lot because he worked overseas. All I wanted to do was sleep and cry. My daughter lived in Ohio with her father and the boys lived with friends or wherever they laid their head. At this point they were grown and doing their own thing. I missed them and traveled to Ohio as often as I could. The depression went on until I spoke to a doctor about my medication and what we needed to do to get me moving again.

May 22, 2012, we took a trip to Aruba and this is where my boyfriend asked me to marry him! Then on June 12, 2012, my boyfriend became my husband. He received a contract that moved us from Fayetteville NC to Tampa, Florida. Around 2014, my husband's daughter and my daughter decided they wanted to live with us full time. I was both excited and scared about this new chapter we were about to enter. I knew it was going to be a challenge, but I was up for it. Chris was still working overseas, so it was good to have the girls around.

I am working on building my speaking and coaching business, Maximum Transformation LLC. This is the year that I will spend time with God and download exactly what he is wants me to do. I have been spinning my wheels, living in fear, thinking I have nothing to offer anyone. Even though God spoke to me about impacting others! What is wrong with me!!! I will step out on faith and walk in the purpose God has placed on my life. I will write more books, I will speak at events, and I will touch many lives! I have had setbacks; however, I refuse to give up. If you have ever faced any type of trauma in the military, don't allow it to paralyze your future. You can do anything you put your mind to, and God has your back. So, look to the hills from whence your help comes from.

A Glimpse At Tech Sgt Hall's Military Life

TAKIYAH KAMILAH HALL

"Fear thou not; for I am with thee: be not dismayed; for I am thy God: I will strengthen thee; yea, I will help thee; yea, I will uphold thee with the right hand of my righteousness."

– (Isaiah 41:10)

In 2000, against my parent's better judgement, I enlisted in the Active Duty United States Air Force. I was 22-years-old and the single mom of a, 2 ½ year old son. I didn't about the consequences of giving sole custody of my son to my parents or the impact that it would on my son and I's relationship. I truly thought that I was doing what was best financially for the both of us. My goal was to go to basic training, send my parents money to care for him, graduate, and wait to be assigned a duty station. After being assigned and moving there, my plans were to get situated, and send for my son. With those plans in mind, I was sworn in at MEPS and given a ship date of March 31, 2000. Taking and passing the ASVAB wasn't the only coal that I had in the fire. I also applied for a sales position with Cellular One, (which became Ameritech; SBC Global, and now AT&T Corporation).

After a couple of weeks, I was called in to interview. My emotions were running high because I was extremely nervous. It was the first time that I had a panel interview of people looking at me at once, hanging on my every word and gesture. It was during that interview that I began to question myself as to why I applied for the job in the first place. "I am not a salesperson; I can't sell a dream, "is what I was telling myself as they stared at me waiting for my answers. I can't remember what I said to those interviewers, but whatever it was, it was enough for them to offer me a full-time position. I breathed a sigh of relief after the offer. A huge boulder had been lifted off my shoulders. I screamed praises at the top of my lungs inside of my vehicle. In my mind, getting a job with them was the best thing that had happened to me in a very long time. It didn't bother me in the least bit when I was told there would be mandatory training for two weeks in a Northern Suburb of Chicago, and that after successfully through it, the job location would be in the city of Chicago. I agreed to the terms and happily accepted the job. A couple of days later, I called my recruiter and told him my good news! I told him something to the effect of "I have been offered a full-time job with good pay and benefits, so I will no longer be joining the Air Force." Of course, he tried to talk me out of my decision, but I wasn't budging. I didn't raise my hand to enlist twice, so I knew I was good, as I chuckled to myself.

From 2000 to 2011 I worked at Cellular One; Ameritech; SBC Global, and AT&T Corporation, wondering if I had made the right decision back in 2000. I kept asking myself where would I be in life if I had joined the Air Force like I initially enlisted and swore in to do? Would I be better off? Worse off? What state or country would I be living in right now? I kept migraine headaches because of the many questions that were filling my head on a daily. To put an end to them, I googled the Air Force once again. I was searching for the cut-off age for active duty, anxiously hoping that I didn't miss it. To my pure disappointment, I missed it by a few years. However, I didn't get discouraged. As I continued to research the branch, I found out that with a degree, I could enlist as a commissioned officer. So, what did I do? Yep, I Googled Air Force officer recruiting offices in Chicago. I found one in my area and gave the office a call. TSgt Full-of-Crap answered my call. I was direct with her and told her that I was looking to join the reserves as an officer. She said okay, took my information and made an appointment with me to come to the office. I was elated.

A week later, I met with her, again reiterating my desire to commission, while confirming that she was the correct person to speak with about it. She made sure to get all my pertinent information before telling me that, "The Air Force longer commissions officers off the streets. You must go enlisted and cross over by way of the deserving Airman program." I took her word for it because after all, she uses integrity always, and has no reason to lie to me, right? She puts service before self, right? How about I was wrong times one million? She only thought about lining her pockets with her commission checks. She absolutely did not use integrity at all, and she most definitely didn't put servicing my needs over hers. As she was typing my information into the computer, she asked me additional questions like, what degrees do you have? What fields are they in? How many credits do you think you have? As I was about to answer her, she interrupted stating that she's asking me those questions because once I graduate from technical school, I will put on E-3 rather than E-1.

In my mind I was thinking, "So I guess that's my consolation prize for not being able to go in directly as an officer?" I smirked while looking at her with my side-eye. She happened to look up and asked me what was my facial gesture about? "Oh, nothing TSgt Full-of Crap" is what I should have said. Instead I asked, can I answer your questions about my degrees now? Lol, yes, I'm sorry," she said. "I have an associates in marketing, a bachelor's in business communications, and I'm months from finishing my master's in business administration." "Wow! Okay, definitely look into the deserving airmen's program to commission in a couple of years," she said. I rolled my eyes. "What jobs are available TSgt?" She answered, "If you are trying to leave as soon as possible, Security Forces is available." What is Security Forces?" I asked. "It's the military police. They secure the base, check id's, carry weapons, and things like that. Is that something you would be interested in?" I said, "Honestly? No, I'm more into administrative jobs, especially because of my degrees." She said, "Yes, I understand that, and you could always cross over, but if you want to leave sooner than later, Security Forces is your way out." "Is there a sign-on bonus for the job," I asked? "No," she said. "They don't give them every year, it depends." Again, I rolled my eyes. I said, "It doesn't sound like enlisting has any benefits for me?" She blabbered on about the "benefits" of enlisting. Because I had already backed out of going 11 years prior, in my mind I was like whatever, and kept the process going.

July 11, 2011, I boarded the plane to San Antonio, Texas as trainee Hall. It was the first day to the beginning of my new life. My mind was flooded with a million emotions. I was scared, happy, sad, frantic, anxious, angry, and inpatient. All I could replay in my mind was my cousin telling me what to expect when I get off the plane. She said they would yell, scream, demean me, embarrass me, curse me out, and make me instantly regret my decision to join the Air Force Reserves. I closed my eyes while listening to music in my playlist at that time, wanting the two-hour, 39-minute flight from Chicago to Texas to be over, anxious of what was to come. Finally, the plane landed. I gave out a huge sigh of relief, gathered my items, and slowly walked to baggage claim to get the rest of my bags. Boy oh boy was I in for a surprise, but not really. My cousin told me that MTI's would seek us out and immediately start their shenanigans. She was right! I could barely get my other bags together before they started yelling, Move! Move! Move! You're moving too slow! You act like you have nowhere to be female! Get your bags! Today! Now! I was so thrown off that I couldn't do anything but laugh.

They were certainly being extra. There was about 50 of us lined up, being yelled at. People came from all over the United States to go to basic training in San Antonio, Texas. We were a diverse group. There were Blacks, Whites, Hispanics, Asians, and Indians. From the moment we were lined up, race was no longer a factor. We were trainees in the military. We were nothings and nobodies to those in charge. They were in a position to treat us less than the dirt on the bottom of their shoes, and there was nothing we could do about it. We were on their turf at that point. It was at that very moment that I instantly regretted enlisting, swearing in twice and getting my 32-year-old behind on the plane to Texas. What was I thinking? What was I trying to prove? Was this the best decision to make? Why? Why? Why? As soon as I thought I could answer my own questions, I was quickly brought back to reality with the MTI's screaming at the top of their lungs telling us to pick up our bags fifty times, drop them back down fifty times, before directing us to get on the bus. Okay good, I can relax for a few minutes on the bus before the night really kicks off, is what I told myself as I found a seat and sat down.

One week later, July 18, 2011, "Boot Camp," was in full force. On this day, I turned 33 years old. Yes, 33! Again, I began to question my reasons for coming into the military at such a seasoned age. And then it hit me, oh yeah, that's why! Because I live for challenges. I want to prove that I can hang with the best of those 18-25-year old's. I wanted to show my son that joining the military is a life-changing event that can be beneficial if you make it work for you. So, on that 33rd day of my life, I woke up with a renewed appreciation for life. I told the ladies on the flight that it was my birthday. They gave me birthday wishes and blah blah blah. However, what I didn't expect was for them to tell our Military Training Instructor (MTI). He didn't tell me happy birthday because of his position, but he made me aware that he knew it was a, "special day,"

He asked my age, and when I told him, his face lit up like a Christmas tree. At that moment, he told me he couldn't tell how old I was, but that I looked younger than I acted. I took it as a compliment because who wants to be told that they look old, but act immature lol. Not me. So, the morning went on and it was time to take the forever minute run around the track. I certainly felt like I was 33 during that time. No matter how much cardio I did prior to coming to boot camp, every morning that we had to run around that track, wore me completely out. My legs felt like jelly, my chest caved in and out as if I had smoked 33 cigarettes. My head was spinning like a

Frisbee, and my arms were all over the place as I tried effortlessly to catch my breath. There were several times I wish I had 18-year-old legs, but nevertheless, I made it through.

One week later, our MTI had a doctor's appointment, so he was given a sub. That sub was the worst human being I had encountered up to that point. He was a master sergeant with five million muscles from his head to his toes. He was a bald white man, but because screaming, which has been his favorite thing to do as a part of his MTI job, red was the color that he can best be identified by. I don't know if he was angry that he had to sub or what his problem was, but on my birthday, he sought me out to pick on. This is what he yelled— What's your name trainee? Why are you here trainee? How old are you trainee? I gave my reporting statement, "Sir Trainee Hall reports as ordered," I am 33. He didn't let me finish answering the questions because he was too busy being fixated on my age. 33? 33?

What does your family think about you joining the military at 33? Aren't they ashamed of you for joining at your age? Aren't you ashamed that you joined at your age? What do you expect to get out of the military at your age? He just went on and on. I was extremely humiliated. How dare this bald head bastard demean me and spew out my age like it's a disease or something? I wanted so badly to kick the crap out of his mouth. Instead, I stood at attention, held my military bearing and about-faced when dismissed.

As the weeks went on, word got around the flights, that a 33-year-old was in the midst. I swear it seemed like all eyes were on me whenever we were around other flights. Clearly, it was my conscience getting to me, or was it that I wasn't acting childish like the 18-year old's? Who knows? I wasn't ashamed of my age, but I was angry that I was older than most of the Military Training Instructors (MTI's) during my time there. All I could think was that, had I not backed out from going active duty in 2011. I would be an officer or NCO at this point and wouldn't be here getting belittled by these super-wack MTI's. So, life dealt me the hand that I played. I made the decision not to join 11 years ago, so this is my punishment.

The last two weeks of boot camp, my Air Force bootcamp military flight was called into a meeting with a female MTI from another flight. She asked us if we had experienced sexual harassment or sexual assault from male flights or MTI's? Many of us said no, but a couple of my flight mates turned beet red and turned their heads. She noticed their behavior and continued with her lecture. When she finished, I saw her pull them to the side. The rest of us were dismissed to start cleaning for the night. At the end of the night, the two females that were pulled to the side by the female MTI earlier, told us in confidence that they knew a few of the trainees who had been involved with their MTI's.

My mouth opened wide with surprise and disgust. I had so many questions. Who were they? How old were they? Who were their MTI's? Where did the incidents happen? How did they kick off to begin with? Was it anal, oral, or vaginal sex? Who gave and who received? My flight mates were overwhelmed after all the questions. They were flustered because I could see it all in their faces. They didn't have many satisfying answers but gave the ones that they could. Turns out, the MTI's would come into the buildings after hours and request to see certain trainees. They would promise them extra phone time, store time, exemption from clean-up, in exchange for sexual favors such as oral and vaginal sex.

The trainees were supposed to keep it to themselves, but come on now, we are talking about females after all. I'm not sure if they told because they were trying to shed light on what they were experiencing as trainees in boot camp, trying to see if other flights were going through it, or if they thought it was okay for them to sleep with their MTI's as a badge of honor? I shudder to think that this would be the case. However, you never really know what is going on in people's minds. All I could think to do was pray for the victims. Regardless of what the reasoning was behind the occurrences, nevertheless, they were victims.

During graduation week, an announcement had been made that the victims of sexual assault would be delayed from graduating due to the ongoing investigation. The male MTI's had since been removed from their positions as well. Female MTI's had been placed in those flights to ensure the safety of the remaining female trainees. Again, I prayed for the victims and their flight mates because they experienced a traumatic event in what should have been a safe environment free of sexual harassment and assault. Especially because we are treated and viewed as nobodies and nothings while in training mode. Since that obviously was not the case, graduation day was bittersweet. It was bitter because of the dark cloud the announcement earlier in the week left, but sweet because my son, my father, my sister, and my ex-mother-in-law, all came to see this 33-year-old airmen graduate from the United States Air Force basic military training. I was extremely happy to see and hear them in the crowds cheering me on. After the ceremony, they ran up to me, nearly knocking me to my feet by aggressively hugging me, telling me how proud they were of me, and wished me words of encouragement.

In January 2012, I attended my first drill weekend at Grissom ARB. I reported to my unit, Security Forces, (military police). Yes, I have a badge and beret to prove it, and yes, I carried two weapons while on duty (M-4 rifle, and M-9 pistol). I wasn't surprised to see a shortage of women in the unit. Let's say out of 150 members, 25 of them were women. We were always singled out. The language used by the men in that unit was degrading and offensive. They would say things like, "Hall, what makes you think you are cut out to do a man's job? Why aren't you in a unit where you can sit behind a desk? Can you even fire a weapon? I can't wait to see what you have to offer this unit, "as a woman." Not many of you stick around, but those who do, serve their purpose." Every time I walked into the room, it felt like I was being undressed down to my bra and panties with their eyes. I felt so violated. Omg! What the heck did I get myself into? I've heard of cops having filthy mouths, and being sexist against women, but damn, this takes the cake on my first day in the unit.

A couple of months into being a part of Security Forces, I began to feel extremely uneasy when reporting to drill. Why? Because I began to witness sexual harassment being done to my female teammates. I became close with a couple of the females and they felt comfortable enough to confide in me. One told me that her supervisor told her he could imagine her giving him oral sex on her knees as he sat in the chair at his desk, in his office. She said that he laughed it off, so she wasn't sure if he was serious or not. I was in such disbelief that he told her that, I didn't even think to ask what was said for him to say it or feel comfortable to let it come out of his mouth to an airman or woman other than his wife at all! I told her laughing or not, that was very unethical, unprofessional, disrespectful, unwarranted, and that she should report him. Since we were new to the unit, she didn't want to "cause" trouble. I told her it's not about causing trouble, it's about reporting unethical behavior by leadership. She never reported it. A year or so later, he was deployed. While overseas, he took that same behavior with him. Unfortunately, a few women fell victim to his tactics of holding his rank over their heads. He was an E-7, and they were E-3 AND E-4'S.

Allegedly, he sexually assaulted them by having them give him oral sex, while having threesomes on multiple occasions. Allegedly, he threatened to demote their rank, if they reported him. Clearly, they did not appreciate being threatened and reported it to senior leadership. After investigating the occurrence, he was initially detained, his deployment orders were cut. Afterwards, he was sent back home to the United States, he was demoted to an E-3, he was discharged other than honorably, his civilian job was notified of his behavior and the events following, and his wife divorced him. He hasn't been seen or heard from since, so the term allegedly may be incorrect at this point. Although I can't say for sure what became of him, I am more than confident that he is regretting all those poor decisions, done all in the name of power and lust.

Time passed as I, "settled," into the unit of sexist men who treated women as unequal, while thinking of them as less than capable of, "doing a man's job." I began to think of an exit strategy because I was convinced that I did not belong there. I started talking to the career adviser about my options. She told me that I could cross train into a more "fitting" career, such as personnel, (human resource management). I was intrigued and excited. However, I did not have the time in grade to qualify to cross-train at the time. My heart sank. My mood shifted to disappointment and I began to feel trapped. I expressed to my supervisor how I was feeling. He seemed to genuinely care about my concerns. He gave me words of encouragement and told me to, "Suck it up airman," as a phrase of endearment. It was supposed to make me laugh, but because of the disappointment I was feeling, I rolled my eyes. As the day went on, he watched my mood and actions closely. Why? I was suicidal and going to verbally attack anyone who said something I didn't like or because I may have vacated the premises without telling anyone? Nope. None of those things was his reason for watching me like a hawk that day. It turns out he was interested in having more than a supervisor/ troop relationship. To prove the point, he looked up my phone number from the recall roster and texted me the next day during lunch.

A female friend and I were walking from my car to the building with McDonald's bags in our hands. I received a text from a number that wasn't stored as a contact. It said, "Why didn't you bring me McDonald's?"

I looked around the parking lot, trying to see who was watching me. Naturally I asked, "Who is this?" The reply was, "Your supervisor." I replied, "Where are you? Why are you watching me? Why did you text me?" Without hesitation, as silly as it may have been to tell her to leave me, I told my friend to go in the building. I went back to my car and called the number. He answered. Turns out he was a few cars ahead of mine. He was taking a nap on his lunch, his alarm woke him up, and he saw us walking after he shut his alarm off.

I was still confused by why he chose my phone number to save to contact me. He stated that he wanted to follow-up with me from the events of the previous day. I was skeptical but went with it because if I had to be honest with myself. I liked the attention, and he was easy on the eyes. He was 6 ft 5 inches tall, with a beige skin tone, and the salt and pepper hair thing going on. Who wouldn't want a random text from a tall, handsome man with that description? If you say you wouldn't, you're lying to yourself. That random lunchtime phone conversation led to years of an off and on, "relationship" between him and I. I soon realized that not only was he tall and handsome, but he was very muscular. The man stayed in the gym. Anyone who knows me, knows I love "buff" men. I love tall men with huge arm muscles and those plump, gym butts.

He was an E-6, and I was an E-3, until I was promoted to E-4. I enjoyed being with him because I had the, "Best of both worlds." During the duty day, I was the subordinate completing tasks assigned to me by my supervisor, but after the duty day was over, I was his, "woman." We would go back to lodging and unwind for the day. We had a routine that worked for us. We would shower together, make love, go to dinner, come back to the room, have sex as a nightcap, and go to bed. He was law enforcement on the civilian side, so he was controlling in the bedroom. He would command me to give him oral sex to the point of almost ejaculating, then tell me to ride him. I would do as I was told partly because I was thrilled at his demands, but most importantly because I loved having sex with him. This "relationship," went on for a few years.

The reason why it was, "off and on," is because during the month, we didn't see each other as much as I would have liked, due to our work and school schedules. We were both single parents, full-time students, and full-time employees at our jobs. So, in my mind, the days that we were both off work or didn't have a whole lot going on, I felt should have been spent with each other. But that was not the case. To sum it up, he simply didn't make time for me. "People make time for the things they want," is the quote I repeated to him over and over again. He would brush me off and tell me I'm tripping. I'm not being supportive. He's doing what he must do to secure his future. I would get frustrated and, "break up" with him quite often. We would make up, and the cycle would continue.

I made mention that it's funny how I could count on seeing him for drill weekends, but it was a guessing game if I would see him during the month. He would get defensive and start talking crazy to me. I would threaten to leave him alone for good, reminding him that I'm a good catch, a good woman with a head on my shoulders, that has no problems getting the attention of men, and that another man would take me more seriously. He would get enraged when I said those things to him. On occasions he would text me pictures of a woman with a bloody head from a gunshot wound, or a picture of a Dodge Challenger that has been crashed to the point of being totaled, or send texts threatening to put my pictures and videos online for everyone to see. I would get so stressed out from the back and forth with him, the threats, and the violent pictures. I ended up searching for free therapy sessions on Military One Stop. I was successful in finding a therapist in my area and was qualified for 10 sessions. However, I only attended six.

During those sessions, I expressed to my therapist what I was going through. I told her about my, "relationship," with my supervisor. I told her how toxic I felt it was, and that I had doubts about our actual status. As I delved more into my business with her over the sessions, getting it off my chest started to make me realize where the root of my issues began. But rather than completing the 10 sessions to ultimately get to the root cause of the issues I was having as an adult, I stopped going. At the time, I wasn't ready to face the truth, so I avoided it.

As time went on, my, "man," decided to leave the military. You may be saying, okay what's wrong with that? If he honored his contract, he has the right to leave when he no longer wants to be there. Those are true statements. However, as I mentioned previously, I was guaranteed to see him on drill weekends, but during the month, it was a gamble. So, with that said, the "relationship," went downhill from there. We broke up for a few months because we didn't see eye-to-eye. Meanwhile, my drill life still went on. It wasn't the same because he wasn't there, but life still had to go on without him so I, "Sucked it up."

In June of 2013, my unit came back from two weeks of weapons training in Southern Indiana. During training, we had to fire every weapon in the armory because there was an excessive amount of ammunition that had to be used before the close of the fiscal year. We had to fire pistols, rifles, machine guns, and grenade launchers. The day that I dreaded the most was weapons cleaning. To my disappointment, it came sooner than I hoped. The day was long and chaotic because of the number of weapons we had to clean. It didn't matter which weapon you fired or didn't fire, they all had to be cleaned. So, being the obedient airman that I was, I did as I was told. I started cleaning the weapons that were handed to me. I started with a M-9 pistol, moved on to a M-4 Rifle, and was then handed a M203 grenade launcher.

As I started the routine to clean it, somehow, I tripped over the strap and it began to fall to the ground. Instead of letting the weapon fall on my steel toe boots, my instinct was to catch it with my hands. Smart right? Not so much. The most traumatic thing happened because of me not using common sense. The grenade launcher landed right in between my index and second finger of my right hand. The impact of the hit broke the bone between those fingers. Ouch! My hand had immediately gotten swollen! I screamed to the top of my lungs! Tears were streaming down my face from the pain the impact of the hit caused. Everyone in the room turned around to see what happened. I could barely get the story out before everyone rushed to my aid. Leadership had my friend to take me down to Med One in Kokomo, Indiana to be seen. They took x-rays of my hand. That's when I found out that my bone had been broken. After spending a couple of hours there, she took me back to the base to report the findings. I was released early.

The 3.5 hour drive back home was dreadful. I could barely keep the steering wheel straight because my dominant hand is my right hand, and I tried my best to drive with it all wrapped up in gauze tape, while trying to avoid bumping it unnecessarily. After what seemed like 3.5 days, rather than hours, I made it home. I made plans to go to the hospital to get a referral for surgery on my hand, and finally got into the bed for a restless night of sleep. Two months later, in August of 2013, I had an appointment for reconstructive surgery. The procedure was successful, but I had no use of my right hand for months. I was not happy about the medical bandage covering my hand, or the sling that my arm rested in. it was quite embarrassing. The pity parties that people gave me were overwhelming to say the least. I am an attention hog to be honest (unless it's from a handsome man of course lol). Needless-to-say, I was grateful that people cared, but annoyed all the same. I was in physical therapy for months until I was able to use it, and as a result, was off work during that time. The rest of 2013 went by in a painful whirlwind because of the injury, therapy and time off from work.

In 2014, I returned to my civilian job. I wasn't happy about it, but I was glad to be able to have limited use of my hand again. As the months went by, I was still recovering, but pressed on. In April of 2014, my sister from another mister, went into the hospital for a minor surgery. She was supposed to have the operation, stay in the hospital for a few days to recover, and then be discharged to go home go fully recover. Unfortunately, the complete opposite happened. She went in for the scheduled operation, experienced a major complication, which resulted in her being hospitalized long-term, sent to a rehabilitation center, experienced another complication.

Eventually, she passed away on July 12, 2014. She was 34 years old and left four daughters behind. Prior to her passing away, God pressed it upon my heart to go see her in the rehabilitation center, Thursday, July 10, 2014 of my drill weekend.

When I walked into the room where she was located, I immediately began to cry. She was laying in the bed looking very helpless, and in chronic pain. She couldn't talk, but she could respond to your questions by moving a finger or toe. I asked her if she knew who I was? She responded. I asked her if she was in pain, she responded. She began to cry uncontrollably, scream, pant, scream, pant, and cry again. I knew she was in pain. I called for a nurse to come to the room to see what was going on. The nurse stated it was time for her meds. She said she would go get them and come right back. I cried and prayed with my sister while waiting for the nurse to return. About 15 minutes passed and she didn't return. I tried my best to sooth my sister by rubbing her hands and feet and telling her she would be okay. I told her that I loved her and that I would continue to pray for her. She looked at me with tears falling down her face. She nodded off to sleep for a few minutes. I prayed for God to take her pain away. As I was praying, she woke up screaming, panting and crying. I tried to calm her down, but she wouldn't stop. I called the nurse again. She came into the room and gave my sister the medications. I thanked her and asked her if my sister would be okay. She said yes, not to worry, and that she was in good hands. I didn't believe her, because they are paid to say that, but I said okay. I told my sister once again that I loved her, I would pray for her recovery and healing and that I had to leave but would be back to see her next week because I had to go to drill. She cried and nodded off. I left the rehabilitation center in tears. I couldn't believe how my sister was being treated, how she kept screaming out, and that she was completely helpless. I vowed to God that I would be back to see her after the drill weekend was over.

Sunday, July 13, 2014, all the shenanigans of my drill weekend came to an end. I had just returned from the medical clinic down in Kokomo, Indiana from being seen for my ear. During the weekend, I experienced hearing loss in one ear, due to all the weapons firing that we did for two days. On top of being deaf in one ear, it had the nerve to be clogged as if I had a ton of wax in it or something. I felt defeated because not only did I have to leave my sister a couple of days prior in excruciating pain, now I can't even hear out of one ear and must take medication for the next couple of days. Ugh! I asked myself, how much longer am I going to be able to do this military thing? Before I could answer, as I was pulling out of the parking lot to turn to leave the base, my mother called me. She asked if I was busy? I hated when she asked me that because what she says following that, is rarely ever good news. I told her that I was about to leave the base. She told me to pull into a parking spot. I knew this couldn't be good. My heart started racing. I asked what was wrong?

She was choked up and sounded like she had been crying. Slowly she said, it's your sister, she passed away last night. My heart dropped that instant. I immediately started crying, shaking, screaming all at the same time. No, no, no, no, no! I cried. Not my sister! How? Why? Oh my God! My mom tried to console me as best she could. It was useless, but I couldn't hold her on the phone, so I stuttered okay and bye at some point. I stayed parked and cried my heart out. After a while, I gathered myself and drove back to my unit. I told the first sergeant what happened. She gave me her condolences, asked me if I would be okay to drive home? I assured her that I would surely try. I left to start my journey. I was a little piggy that day because I cried all the way home.

The weeks and months after her death, seemed to pass by in a blur. I had crying spurts off and on, as well as periods of sadness. A few months later, the little ray of sunshine that I got after that horrific tragedy was being transferred to the personnel, (Human Resources Management), unit after recommendations from leadership in security forces. When I got to my new unit, I was welcomed with open arms. My new leadership was encouraging, knowledgeable, and willing to help me fit in any way possible, and walked me through the process necessary to go to tech school to train for my new career.

I was glad that I was finally doing something in the fields that my degrees were in. I began to flourish in my new unit. I was promoted to an NCO within months of cross-training. I started helping my airmen with their upgrade training.

I became a mentor to my airmen because I could relate to the issues that they were facing in their military careers or in their personal lives. I became the go-to NCO for lots of things in my unit. Because of my winning personality, willingness to aid and assist others, knowledge of job duties, and commitment to the mission of the military, leadership chose to send me on a one-year tour to Stuttgart, Germany.

My one-year tour was a blessing. The mission was to combat against narcotic operations. In addition to my primary duties, I was able to involve myself with organizations to display my leadership, mentorship, and fellowship skills. I volunteered for several additional duties during the duty day, to help with the mission and to make my home unit proud. The USO was my favorite organization to volunteer in, outside of the duty day. There were always activities like food giveaways happening that required my time. It felt good to give back to military members and their families.

Although I was homesick and missed my family and friends, being around others who were in similar situations, helped. I also volunteered to be a Sexual Assault Prevention and Response victim advocate. I was able to mentor those who experienced trauma while being overseas.

Being stationed in Germany also had travel perks. Because I was in the middle of Europe, I was able to travel to several countries in my down time. I went to other parts of Germany to tour their castles, see the Berlin Wall, the Holocaust cemetery, other historic landmarks, Amsterdam, Spain, Greece, France, Italy, and England. I enjoyed every country that I went to. I was able to see and experience their cultures versus just seeing it on television. I was and still am grateful for the leadership in my unit sending me to Germany for that tour. I gained skills and experience that I was able to bring back to my unit. I am now an E-6 in the reserves and am eligible to sew on E-7 in April of 2020.

I have faced many obstacles in my civilian and military life since enlisting in January of 2011, but I do not regret my decision. I have accomplished getting several degrees, ranking-up in a short period of time, witnessing my son establish a successful career in the Navy, getting hired for two federal service positions, meeting very influential mentors along the way, meeting the love of my life, joining two very prominent and successful sororities, and writing my chapter of life in this book with four other beautiful, successful, honorable, and admirable women.

"And keep the charge of the LORD thy God, to walk in his ways, to keep his statutes, and his commandments, and his judgments, and his testimonies, as it is written in the law of Moses, that thou mayest prosper in all that thou doest, and whithersoever thou turnest thyself:"

- (1 Kings 2:3)

Coming to L.I.F.E

VANESSA SINGLETON-FOULKS

"I shall not die, but I shall live and recount the deeds of the Lord."
Psalm 118:17 (ESV)

With a 9mm Glock in my hands, I knew that the only way out was to fix this situation myself. As I slowly loaded the magazine, the voices rang loudly in my mind, voices of disappointment and failure. I should leave and not look back, (push, slide). But I have no money, (push, slide). My sons would be better with my mom, (push, slide). If I just disappeared, no one would notice, (push, slide). Who would believe me anyway, (push...slide)? As I contemplated ending my life, I wanted them to find my body in a clean apartment. I washed the dishes, vacuumed the floors, made my bed, hung up all my clothes, showered and put on my favorite sweat-suit. I sat down on the floor in the middle of my bedroom, tears running down my face, that made stains of wetness on my sweats. "God don't let my sons be anything like me, and don't let them remember me," I said.

I lifted the gun to my mouth, pointing the barrel upward against my chin, rationalizing a plan to count to three. I moved my finger and placed it on the trigger, still sobbing. I shifted to lean against the foot of the bed and closed my eyes. It will be quicker in my mouth, I adjusted and put the barrel in my mouth as I sobbed quietly, I began to say, "I'm sorry Mommy, I'm sorry Demetrius, I'm sorry Osei." I applied pressure with my sweaty finger on the trigger and...my phone rang.

My son said, "Hi Mommy, when are you coming to get us? I miss you so much, are you still playing with guns?" My oldest son saved my life, and he didn't even know it. I said, "Hi Mechy, I'll see you in three days, son. What are you doing? Where's Grandma?" It amazes me that to this day, 20+ years later, my child called me at the exact time I was trying to kill myself. I always believed he could read my mind. "Mommy, are you crying? God said you can't leave me." And just like that, I remembered that my sons needed me, loved me, and relied on me. I'm their mother; I'm supposed to fight for them; and, take care of them and protect them. Protect them from everything that would hurt and destroy them. I couldn't run from life, I had to stay and fight, if not for me, then for them. The military was not always dark for me, I now, consider it the best, yet the most challenging time of my life. It didn't automatically get better right away, and I had to deal with what drove me to the point of wanting death more than life.

So, to start at the beginning, I heard about the United States Army from a cousin. He and his wife did awesome work in the Army. He was a Warrant Officer and she, a Commissioned Officer. They went through the ranks quickly. So, once I had my oldest son and made a plan for our lives, the Army became that plan. On June 12, 1996, I kissed my baby boy, hugged my mother and left for Basic Training at Fort Jackson in South Carolina. I had never been away from my mother, and son; and, honestly, nothing could have prepared me for those experiences. We had to train, train and train even more. I thought these people were crazy, up at 0400, shared showers, 50+ roommates and never enough privacy. Being the introvert that I *was*, these living, sleeping and eating arrangements were stretching me out of my comfort zone.

For the first time ever, I had to speak up and take care of myself, if I wanted to survive these eight weeks. I am actually grateful for this time; it taught me discipline, teamwork and looking out for my battle buddies (those Soldiers to my left and right). In some cases, to look out for people who, outside of the military would consider lynching someone like me, and here I was telling them what to do. I am not saying that the military does not have any racist, but that old mindset is hard to break when the one you didn't give any power to, now has power over you. I can, specifically, recall one young lady from Mississippi who would always pick the black girls to clean the toilets. She would never shower, or use the bathroom after the black girls, and she stated, we should be separated, when we ate. One morning, while I was handing out the assignments, for the evening cleaning, she sees her name on the latrine (bathroom) duty. She decides to tell another young lady to inform me she doesn't clean bathrooms. I respond, "Well tell her to come talk to me about it and I'll see what we can do." The soldier, looked at me with an embarrassed look, and mumbled under her breath, "She doesn't talk to people like you, that's why I am asking you." I instantly looked up from my task and asked, "People like me? What does that mean?" So here I am a native New Yorker in the middle of the South, not grasping the concept that this chick didn't like me because I was black. I could not recall not one time I had to deal with racism as a child or as an adult. "So, what does that mean?" I asked again, "Like you- you are a nigger," was her reply.

Although she was obviously trying to lower her tone, it seemed as if everyone in the room heard her and the background talking and chatter that was once present was now gone. As I stared at this 18- year-old white girl, with rage, I could see out of the corner of my eye, the room suddenly divide. It was like a scene in a movie. The brown and black females were slowly walking to the side of the room that I was on and the white females were moving in the opposite direction. It was as if they just knew this was about to be a heated altercation. Being the analytical person that I am, so many thoughts were running through my mind. Like, I should slap the shit out of her and let her know how a nigger do. I'm about to send this chick home in a box, right back to the racist people she came from. But all I could think was, this bitch tried me. Remembering that I was the oldest person in this class and that I was someone's mother pulled me back to reality that I did not want to go to jail. "Well if she can't come talk to *this* nigger about her issue, then I guess she will be cleaning toilets," is all I could muster up to say. As a matter of fact, after the anger, I was hurt. I felt the tears welling up in my eyes, but I fought them back, so no one would know. She just stood there and looked at me, I said, "Is there something else?" I wanted out of there, out of the military, who in the hell did she think I was? My mother doesn't even call me names.

"No, I guess not. I'll let her know," was her reply.

The talking and chatter seemed to pick right back up where it left off and the incident was over. I, on the other hand, was not back to normal. I went to a stairwell on the back side of the building and cried out all my anger, hurt, and embarrassment. I wiped my face and nose and went back to the day. Needless to say, that young female did clean those toilets. But I was there with her cleaning them as well, I wanted to prove to her that I was no different than her. No matter what she thought of me because of the color of my skin. My reaction did not affect her too much, or so I thought, but her "messenger" friend started consulting me for guidance on every task for the remainder of our time there. At graduation as I hugged and kissed my baby boy, I could see out of the corner of my eye, they were staring at me. Both of the females came over to me and wished me good luck. I introduced them to my family and my son. I was taken aback when the young lady gave me a hug and walked away. Wow! I often think of my reaction to them on that first day and thank God I responded and not reacted. That would have been ugly...

My first duty station was Ft. Sill, Oklahoma, this included my first apartment and my first car. So many responsibilities thrown on me at once was a bit overwhelming, but I loved every bit of it. I went to clubs, drank alcohol, met great people and had money of my own. The military created a woman out of me. As I think about it now, I think I went wild once I left my mother's house. Things I was not allowed to do, was now free game to me. I drank and drank a lot, but what I really enjoyed was going to the club and dancing for hours. Dancing gave me a buzz that the alcohol didn't give me. Upon entering the door until leaving at the wee hours of the morning, I was on the dance floor. I couldn't explain the feeling. It wasn't the attention from men because most of the time I was dancing by myself. It wasn't the place because it was a hole in the wall. It was a release of sorts, I felt free. This is where I met my first husband, a fellow Soldier in my unit that always seemed to be in the same circles I was in. From movie night in the barracks to hanging out in the club, we developed a friendship that turned into more. He was a club-head like me and when we danced. OMG! Whenever we danced, especially when reggae was played, our connection was evident. People would watch us, it was like we were the only two people on the floor. It seemed as if we saw each other all day, every day. But he had a girlfriend and a baby back in Georgia that I knew existed, so I wanted to stay friends. I was not into breaking people up or disrupting homes, this was a temporary situation and within two years, we would go our separate ways. But as time went on and we continued to hang out, eventually, we developed feelings. Shortly thereafter, I became pregnant, and, we got married.

Simultaneously of me enjoying life clubbing and meeting my husband, my work life was stressful. I was a mechanic within a Medical Field Hospital. Not being able to keep up with the other "male" mechanics was a challenge. Things they already knew when they came into the military about vehicles, I was just learning. My first year, I hated going to the Motor pool because I knew I was going to be treated bad for being a female. It was as if I didn't belong within this world. I was harassed all around. Harassed for being a female, harassed for being a curvy female, and harassed for not knowing enough about my military occupation. At this time, the Army didn't technically have a process in place for harassment, but if they did, I would have been reporting all the men in my unit on a daily basis. There were constant stares, whispers, comments, and advances. I knew from the age of 16, that I had a big butt and wide hips, but never knew it would bring me so much unwanted comments and glares. This also bought unwarranted meetings and write-ups. It was almost as if I was being punished for being a shapely woman. So, I started to change to fit in with my male counterparts.

My language changed, I drank more, and attempted to erase all aspects of femininity that I had. When I became pregnant and got married, it calmed down a lot, like men knew I was taken. But as soon as people heard I was divorced it was back to what I began to believe was normal. I had to do twice as much work, ace my physical fitness test, work longer hours and prove myself in all areas of life. This was a frustrating time in my life as I never felt good enough. It was as if anything I did wasn't good enough. As if the simple fact that I was a woman made me less than....... a human.

This continued throughout most of my military career, and only got worst until 2003. I deployed to Iraq in 2001-2003. It was so very stressful. I was new to my unit and most of my unit was already in Kuwait. I arrive to the camp at 2 o'clock in the morning and they were waiting for me. The next day I was introduced to everyone. To my surprise I was not the only female in the section. There were 2 other females an older white woman, a specialist (E-4) and an older black woman, a staff sergeant (E-6). "How long you been a 63B, Specialist?" my platoon sergeant asked. "About 3 and a half years, Platoon Sergeant," I stated. "So, you should be good and broken in, right?" with the wink of his left eye, I knew what "good and broken in" meant. I avoided him like the plague, but there was always a meeting or counseling that I had to go to with just him. I could feel his eyes burning through my clothes and as I walked away there was no doubt he was gawking. Sometimes he would even make a comment, "I wonder how wet that would get," or "I just want to cup that ass in my hands and hit that thang from the back" Loud enough so I could hear but soft enough that no one else could hear. I would ask the other females in the section if they experienced awkward moments with him, but there was a negative response. Then they would be shocked as if he couldn't possible be so disgusting. At this unit I was promoted to the rank of Sergeant, got the maximum amount of points on my physical fitness test and won numerous distinguished Soldier awards. Anytime a tasking came down the chain of command, I volunteered. Some thought I was trying to be a "Hooah, Hooah Soldier," when I was just trying to get away from the intimidation and threat that I faced daily.

I felt like I was losing my mind, after returning from Iraq. The dead burnt bodies where all I could dream about. I would wake up sweaty, fighting at the air and scared. Living in this apartment alone was not helping either. I could hear every foot step walking, every shower running, every person snoring and every time someone sneezed hard. The walls were paper thin. But I had ten days and I would be home with my babies, my heartbeats, and my lifelines. One night about 5 days from block leave, I was in my apartment reading a book. I could hear knocking on several doors, that seemed to go unanswered. After about 10 seconds of the fourth knock, the next knock was at my door. I froze thinking, if I don't answer they will go away. "Open up Singleton, I know your there, everybody else is at the club." In a confused state I said, "Platoon Sergeant?????Is that you????" I was really trying to figure out why was he here? At my apartment? What was going on? I didn't hesitate but opened the door. He was *drunk!* He basically fell into my apartment and onto me. The dude had to be about as big as a grizzly bear and about as heavy as one as well. We fell onto the floor. BAM!!! I hit my head on the floor. I think I may have blacked out for a few seconds, because I did not hear what he was saying until he started yelling. "Answer me, you want this dick, Bitch?" I could not figure out what was happening. *Slap,* "I'm gonna show you," *Slap,* "who's in charge," *Slap.* With every slap to my face he was moving his body as if he was thrusting into me. My mind was a blank, my hands and arms where doing their own thing, fighting hard to get away. As we fought, I would try and scoot up from under him, but it was no use. His weight had me pinned down. So, with my door wide open and me crying and fighting on the floor, he ripped my shorts and panties and raped me. I was not naked, my clothes where stretched out so much they were pushed to my side, somehow. He then got up and shut my door. All I could do was cry and lay there, I know I heard the door close and I assumed he was on the outside. But there he was looking at me. "You want some more?" I got up and with all the strength I could muster, I looked him in the eye and said, "Get the fuck out." He stumbled around, saying he going to need a key so he won't have to knock, can we go get something to eat, and if I enjoyed it. Without saying a word and my shorts falling to my ankles, I walked into my bedroom, straight to my closet and reached for the 9mm Glock, I just bought the day before. I could still hear him saying slick shit as I was walking back to the living room. I raised the gun up and pointed it at him. He shuffled back toward the closed door so fast, he fell backwards onto the floor. "GET THE FUCK OUT!"

From a little girl, I have heard people say that everything happens for a reason. I can't say I believe that, because my question would be, Why? This assault made me feel like a failure. How could I let this happen? Why did I open the door? If I told anyone would they even believe me? What would I do now? The next day was Saturday and I slept most of the day, when I did wake up the bruises on my face, legs and arms reminded me of what happen. I could still smell the aroma of liquor, cologne and cigar on my skin, although I showered numerous times. Then Sunday I made up in my mind that I would leave this earth.

I'm not sure how I made it through my time there, but I did. I felt physical pain in my body whenever I had to see him. I changed to another company within the unit and pushed on to do 10 more years in the military. If not for my health, I probably would still be active. I am grateful that Spirit saved my life, through my son. I wrestled with the fact that another person seemed to have taken my strength, my hope and my voice but in retrospect, I have discovered these things. I am not as quiet as I use to be, and I have confidence to stand up for those that may feel as if their voice has been stolen. As a Rape victim advocate, I have cried with and consoled many people that have endured a sexual assault. At first it was like reliving my assault with every interview. But now I see it as me having a voice for those that may not be able to articulate the trauma at the time.

As I gave a slight glimpse into some of the obstacles I've overcome, I am proud to see that time is progressing and measures are put in place for people that are racist, sexist or discriminate in anyway. I hope my story will help someone combat feelings of failure, embarrassment and helplessness.

KATHY R. SMITH
Chandelier Transformations Coaching, Speaking and Writing

Kathy R. Smith, MSHRM is the Founder and President of Chandeliers for Christ a youth mentoring nonprofit organization here in the Tampabay area. She is the "Transformation Strategist", Founder and CEO of Chandelier Transformations Coaching, Speaking and Writing), Motivational Coach and Speaker of John Maxwell Team and International Association of Women as well as a published author. She has appeared on Lens of Faith Speaks talk show.

Kathy is a disabled Army Veteran who has served over 17+ years in United States Army. She is also a Sexual Assault Victim Advocate, Equal Opportunity Leader, Security Manager and a Brand Ambassador for We Are Women of Substance and L.I.F.T (Ladies Intentionally Following Through).

Kathy is also the wife of Retired Command Sergeant Major Anthony Smith, mother of a blended family of 7 children (3 being her own biological children) and a survivor of domestic violence and sexual abuse.

Military award recipient of the Army Commendation Medal, Army Achievement Medal x 2, Good Conduct Medal x2, Army Reserve Component Achievement Medal x6, National Defense Service Medal, Armed Forces Expeditionary Medal x2, Armed Forces Reserve Medal with Meritorious Service, Global War on Terrorism Expeditionary Medal, Global War on Terrorism Service Medal, Armed Forces Service Medal, Armed Forces Reserve Medal, Non Commissioned Officer Professional Development Ribbon x2, Certificate of Appreciation x 4, Army Service Ribbon, Army Overseas Ribbon, Army Reserve Component Overseas Ribbon x2 and numerous plaques and coins of excellence for dedicated service to the United States Army and Army Reserve.

Kathy R. Smith has a passion to help women that have suffered abuse, trauma, hostile work environment, professional and emotional burn-out, low self-esteem and a myriad of other issues that plague women that have served in the Armed Forces and professional women overcome physical, mental and emotional barriers to transform that hurt and pain into lives filled with prosperity and abundance. She strives to instill excellence in young minority females by mentoring them on leadership, self- esteem, healthy relationships and boundaries and educational and Christian values to become pillars of success in their communities.

Kathy holds a Bachelor of Science in Business Administration (Cum Laude) and a Master of Science in Human Resource Management. She is currently pursuing a PhD in Industrial/ Organizational Psychology. Kathy is the lead author of, "Unleashing the Roar" to be released January 2020 and a co-author on her first anthology "We Are Women of Substance".

She enjoys meditating and studying holistic medicine and natural health remedies as well as spending time with her family and friends. She loves seafood and her favorite verse is Jeremiah 29;11 "For I know the plans I have for you declares the Lord, plans to prosper you and not to harm you, plans to give you hope and a future."

CHAUNDRA N. GORE
LensofFaith Speaks

Chaundra Nicole Gore, MSL is a Radio talk show host on the Encouraging Yourself Show on All Nations Stellar Award Winning Radio station, Host of Thursday Night at 8 with LensOfFaith LIVE on Facebook/YouTube, leadership strategist, destiny catalyst, international speaker, motivational coach, ghostwriter, Amazon bestselling author, the Founder and CEO of Lens of Faith Photography LLC, Lens of Faith Speaks and Discovering You Motivational Coaching Program. She is a disabled Army Veteran who has served over 19+ years in United States Army. Chaundra is also a Sexual Assault Victim Advocate, Moderator for Cultivating Clarity in our Community for Domestic Violence, a member Kappa Epsilon Psi Military Sorority Incorporated, an advocate for Service members as a member of The Association for United States Army, Brand Ambassador for We Are Women of Substance, Brand Ambassador for L.I.F.T (Ladies Intentionally Following Through), Brand Ambassador for Black Women Handling Business, and Brand Ambassador for Unstoppable Black Women. Outside of all of her professional titles, she is also a wife, a mother, and a survivor of domestic violence and sexual abuse.

Military award recipient of the Meritorious Service Medal x 3, Army Commendation Medal x 5, Army Achievement Medal x 2, Certificate of Appreciation x 4, Certificate of Excellence x 2 and numerous plaques and coins of excellence for my dedicated service to the United States Army and Army Reserve.

She is currently married and they have a blended family of seven children. Chaundra's passion is to help heal people who have suffered abuse, trauma, low self-esteem, doubt, and fear and provide resources and tools to help them heal and grow.

Chaundra has a Bachelor's of Science in Business Management. A Master's of Science in Leadership. Currently a Doctoral Student at Grand Canyon University pursuing (Organizational Leadership). Chaundra has been featured in "The Untold Chronicles" Magazine (May 2019 Edition). She has been interviewed on the Dr. Jason Carthen Show, All Nations Stellar Award Winning Show, I Am Just Nia Morning Show, Lady Kay Chat Show and Triumph Services – Women Transformed. Chaundra authored her first book January 2019 "I Am A Lens Of Faith", after becoming a co-author on her first anthology "We Are Women of Substance". She is also a co-author in "Lift, Launch, Lead", "Unleashing the Roar" and co-author in "100 Words of Inspiration". She wrote the foreword in "The Healing Journey" and "My Storm, My Story".

She enjoys shopping for shoes and purses. Her favorite food is lobster. She loves seafood. Her favorite quote is, "I Have a Dream", by Dr. Martin Luther King, Jr. and she is an avid book reader.

DIANE ADAMS

Diane Adams, MCM is a transformational coach as the CEO and Founder of Maximum Transformations, LLC. She is also a Notary Republic, public speaker, first time author, a member of Kappa Epsilon Psi Military Sorority, Incorporated serving as a big sister and on the membership committee, and a United States Army Disabled Veteran of sixteen years.

Military award recipient of the Army Commendation Medal x 2, Army Achievement Medal, Good Conduct Medal x2, National Defense Service Medal, Global War on Terrorism Service Medal, Armed Forces Service Medal, and a host of other service ribbons and certificates of achievement.

She is currently married to Chris and together they have a blended family of four children: William, Jr (28), Donavyn (25), Charese (16) and Kristan (15). She is the proud grandmother of a six-year-old grand baby. Diane's passion is and has always been to encourage others and help them realize everything they need is already in them.

Diane has two Bachelor's degrees from Franklin University in Human Resource Management and another in Business Administration. She also has two Master's degrees one in Marketing and another in Communications.

Diane, was born on May 22, 1969 on an Air Force base in Abilene, Texas. Raised by her mother, her and her oldest sister resided in Columbus, Ohio, until she turned 16, at that point she ran away from home. Always an ambitious, determined child, she ran away and ended up in Greensboro, North Carolina.

TAKIYAH K. HALL

Takiyah K. Hall is a child of God and is a true believer in the Lord and Savior Jesus Christ. She is a decorated United States Air Force veteran, who has proudly served since 2011 - as a Non-Commissioned officer. During her time on active duty, she was deployed to the European Command in Stuttgart, Germany to assist with combating counter narcotic operations throughout Europe and Eastern Asia. While in Germany, she became a Sexual Assault Prevention and Response victim advocate, to aide those who experienced traumatic events while serving overseas. She continues to serve her country as a reservist – mentoring and molding airmen to become future non-commissioned officers, and a Veteran Service Representative assisting Veterans to obtain compensation and medical benefits.

She has an associate's degree in Marketing, Criminal Justice, and Human Resource Management; a bachelor's degree in Business Communications; a master's degree in Business Administration; and is currently pursuing her doctorate degree in Business Administration with a concentration in Entrepreneurship. She is a soror and a mentor of The Lady Doves Sorority, and Kappa Epsilon Psi Military Sorority Inc.

She is an avid believer that all things happen for a reason--sometimes that reason is you. By telling her story, she hopes to inspire readers to make decisions that will produce positive outcomes for their lives.

She raised her son Armand E. Paty, as a single parent, with the help of her supportive family and friends.

VANESSA L FOULKS

Vanessa L Foulks is the CEO of Healthy Foulks, a health and wellness company. Vanessa is an ordained minister of God. She is a decorated United States Army veteran, that proudly served for 14 years— as a Senior Non-Commissioned officer, until separating in 2014. During her time on active duty she was deployed to the Eastern Asia to assist with the war campaigns: Operation Enduring Freedom/Operation Iraqi Freedom. Now, she continues to serve her country, as a Veteran Service Representative assisting Veterans to obtain compensational and medical benefits. Furthermore, she is the point of contact for Military Sexual Trauma claims.

She has a Bachelor's degree in Healthcare Administration, a Master's degree in Christian Ministry, and, is, currently, pursuing a Doctor of Education with an emphasis in Organizational Leadership.

She is a speaker and advocate of suicide prevention and sexual abuse issues. She believes that by telling her own story of wrestling with suicide and overcoming sexual abuse, she can help someone to heal, but to become better in life.

She is married to the Rev. Dr. Brian Foulks and the have a blended family of 5 children.